Young Athletes' Blueprint for Mental Toughness

Train the Mind like a Muscle with Simple Daily Routines to Build Focus, Confidence, and Grit

By Ahi Daniels

© **Copyright** _____ 2026 - **All rights reserved.**

The content contained within this book may not be reproduced, duplicated, or transmitted without direct written permission from the author or the publisher.

Under no circumstances will any blame or legal responsibility be held against the publisher or author for any damages, reparation, or monetary loss due to the information contained within this book. Either directly or indirectly. You are responsible for your own choices, actions, and results.

Legal Notice:

This book is copyright-protected. This book is for personal use only. You cannot amend, distribute, sell, use, quote, or paraphrase any part of the content within this book without the consent of the author or publisher.

Disclaimer Notice:

Please note that the information contained within this document is for educational and entertainment purposes only. Every effort has been made to present accurate, up-to-date, and reliable, complete information. No warranties of any kind are declared or implied. Readers acknowledge that the author is not engaging in the rendering of legal, financial, medical, or professional advice. The content within this book has been derived from various sources. Please consult a licensed professional before attempting any techniques outlined in this book.

By reading this document, the reader agrees that under no circumstances is the author responsible for any losses, direct or indirect, which are incurred as a result of the use of the information contained within this document, including, but not limited to, errors, omissions, or inaccuracies.

Table of Contents

Building your Mental Edge 4

Chapter 1: Laying the Groundwork of Mental Toughness 11

Chapter 2: Focus and Attention 37

Chapter 3: Emotional Regulation and Arousal Control 59

Chapter 4: Confidence, Identity, and Self-Talk 88

Chapter 5: Motivation and Goal Architecture 108

Chapter 6: Habits, Sleep, and Physical Foundations 131

Chapter 7: Decision Making and Game Intelligence 150

Chapter 8: Adversity, Injury, and the Comeback Mindset 169

Conclusion: From Blueprint to Daily Practice 189

Appendices 194

Ahi Daniels

Building your Mental Edge

What a player does in the half-second after a mistake determines the next half-season.

I learned that the hard way.

The final minutes of the playoffs. The highlight of my high school basketball career. We were tied, the crowd's tension barely contained, and all I had to do was make that safe pass to my teammate. He was right there by the net. This was simple. Routine. I'd done it a thousand times.

That split-second I thought, "This is simple!" was when I rushed it. When I threw the ball, something felt off in the way it slipped my fingers. I watched, horrified, as it sailed wide and landed right in the other team's hands.

Right then, everything inside me froze. Instead of snapping back into focus, instead of sprinting to recover, I hesitated. I stared at the turnover as if it were a crime scene. In that hesitation, the other team scored.

We lost.

Not only on the scoreboard, but the loss was in my head. For weeks after, I carried that mistake like a mark of shame, replaying it over and over. I doubted myself in practice. I played without confidence. And the rest of my season, I became half a player, performing at half my ability.

That's when it hit me:

Every athlete makes mistakes. The difference between an average player and an elite one isn't the mistake itself—it's the immediate response afterwards. That is where focus, resilience, and mental toughness matter most and shape the entire season.

That moment is where mental toughness resides.

I chose the wrong path in that game. I wasn't mentally tough in that moment. I want *you* to be different.

If you're reading this book, you want more than flashes of greatness—you want true consistency and mental resilience under pressure. This book's goal is to help you become the athlete who performs at your best no matter what.

That's the right move.

If this book does one thing, it's to show you how to stay mentally locked-in, regardless of setbacks. Each chapter offers targeted drills and routines to help you remain focused and unshakeable, so your mind is as disciplined as your skills.

Every concept is grounded in evidence-based techniques drawn from sport psychology, neuroscience, and real coaching experience. These ideas have been tested in the field, in the gym, and under pressure.

By the end of this book, you'll have:

- Immediately usable drills (3 to 7 minutes max) that train focus, relaxation, and recovery.
- Coach/parent scripts to help your support team reinforce your mindset without inadvertently adding pressure.
- Methods to turn mental practice into daily habits to build consistency and sustainability.
- Insights into how to challenge yourself through constraints, encouraging constant improvement, and leveling up.

Those small wins are rooted in daily micro-habits—the true proponents of transformation.

Significant changes don't happen overnight. They occur in the moments you repeat every day. Here, you'll learn to break mental training down into small, simple actions that stack up into visible results. This might mean doing a 3-minute focus reset before practice, or a 5-breath recovery drill after a long game. You might even journal one line about what you learned from a mistake instead of spiraling into self-doubt.

These habits will develop your intrinsic motivation (you'll learn all about that later) and build momentum.

This isn't a theory for me. I've lived and coached these practices.

For years, I coached youth teams in multiple sports, including soccer and basketball, and served as an assistant coach for football and volleyball. I saw kids who had all the talent in the world freeze under pressure, while others with average skills came through when it mattered most.

It got me thinking: *why?* I went down the proverbial rabbit hole of sports research, worked alongside sport psychologists, met with performance consultants, and elite coaches. Together, we uncovered systems that helped athletes strengthen their *mental* game through practice.

Dozens of young athletes used these methods to transform their performance. They didn't magically stop feeling nervous or stop making mistakes. But they *learned how to work those nerves*, to use every mistake as data.

Let me tell you about 14-year-old Andrew.

Talented, fast, strong, intelligent—the quintessential "natural" athlete on paper. But Andrew had a problem; whenever the game was on the line, he froze. Every fourth quarter, it was the same pattern: fumbles, mistakes, frustrations, then shutting down. His teammates stopped passing to him in crunch time. He'd sulk about it, internalizing all those mistakes, hating the competition, the game, and everything else in those moments.

When we started working together, I could've told him to "just be confident," "no pain, no gain," "hustle harder," or "give me 110%." None of those words would have meant anything to him. What we did instead was build small daily routines. His first assignment was a 3-minute **reset drill**: take one deep breath, focus on a keyword ("Next"), and picture the next play. We added a micro-goal each week, like staying vocal after a mistake or using a visualization before tip-off.

After eight weeks, Andrew didn't suddenly become fearless. However, he no longer spiraled after making mistakes. He bounced back within seconds. Even his teammates noticed and began to trust him again, rallying around his improvement and being inspired to work on their own shortcomings. By the end of the season, Andrew got multiple 3-pointers in a clutch game—a goal he'd always wanted to achieve.

That's an inspirational story, but what is this book really about? What does mental toughness *actually* mean?

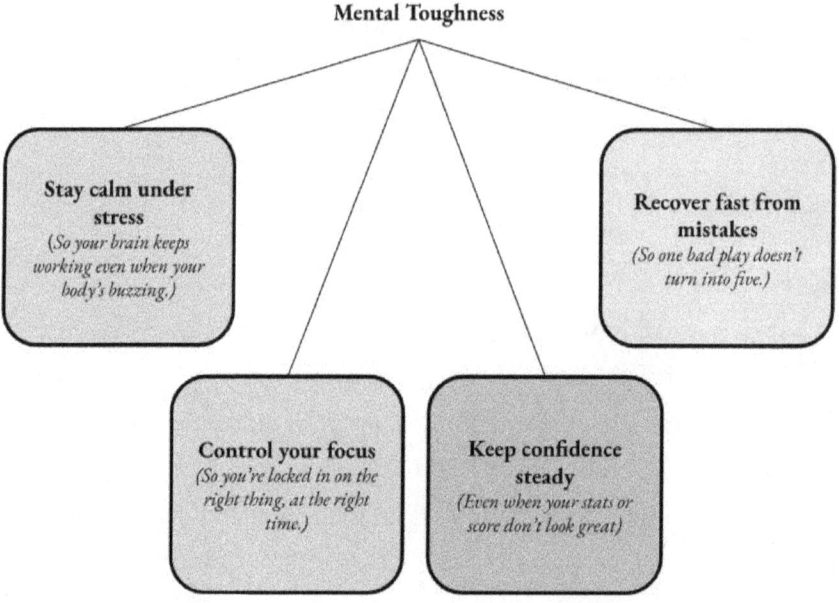

These are all trainable skills, just like shooting, sprinting, or lifting. You weren't born with the perfect jump shot. You practiced. And that's what you need to do for mental toughness.

Now, you have the proper drills, feedback, and systems.

This is a playbook, a guide for you to *use*, not just some light reading. Each chapter explains one key pillar of mental toughness, shows you the research behind it, splits the data into actionable sections designed for busy athletes and teams, and then gives you:

1. Drills you can start immediately.

2. Reflection prompts to track your growth.
3. Measurement tools (like baseline tests or focus trackers).
4. Coach/parent scripts to build your support system.

By the end, you'll be building toward a 30-day micro plan that'll help you build habits step by step.

No one becomes mentally tough by accident. The best athletes, from pros to high school captains, all train their minds, and their key ingredient is *consistency*. That's where you come in. You've already made the first move: deciding to train your mental game as seriously as your physical one. It's time to act.

You don't have to wait until next season or your next tournament. You don't even have to wait until you finish the book! The next page kicks you off with a Micro-Start: three simple drills you can do today in less than ten minutes total!

Micro Start

The Reset

For recentering after a mistake or distraction.

- Take three deep breaths.
- Say one focus cue word: "Ready."

Pre-Training Ritual

Mentally rehearsing responding to pressure with control and grounding composure.

- Quick goal statement ("I will maintain my focus for a full drill.")
- Visualize the first drill carried out smoothly.
- Take an anchoring breath (quick inhale, long exhale).

Evening Reflection

Using your own words to solidify your values and progress.

- Write down one thing you've learned today.
- Write down one thing you improved on.

Chapter 1: Laying the Groundwork of Mental Toughness

There weren't many people out there who thought I could do it. I always thought I could. That's why I busted my butt. The day I believed I couldn't pitch in the big leagues was the day I would quit.

These are the words of one young baseball player. Here, we see the two sides of every athlete and competitor: the work they put in *and* the mental toughness they must maintain.

You see, mental toughness isn't something you're born with. It's something you build.

One rep, one thought, one belief at a time.

Despite what he's been told, what others say, or even what the scoreboard says at the end of a game, mental toughness is what keeps him coming back to the field. It's not about being certain that he will win every time or that everyone believes in him. *He* knows, deep in his heart, mind, and body, that he can climb higher, that he has what it takes. That mental strength is invaluable to taking him every step further.

Sports are a physical endeavor—there's no denying that. However, people often forget the mental aspects that go into it. Stress, training, losses, competition, anger, frustration, joy, triumph; all these are mental and emotional processes that can't be separated from your journey as an athlete. The mind, the home to all this, needs training just like the body does.

You wouldn't walk into the gym and expect to bench 200 pounds on your first day. So, why do we expect athletes to handle high-pressure moments, losses, and emotional swings without practice?

As you go through this book, you'll discover that mental toughness isn't blind confidence. It's the kind of "muscle memory" that keeps your performance sharp and your spirits unbreakable. The mental side of sports isn't something you can simply ignore or forego. According to Weinberg and Gould (2019), in opponent-based sports, performance is about 50% mental, whereas in individual sports it can reach 80-90% (p. 342).

So, no, mental toughness *isn't* a personality trait, but a skillset that can be learned, measured, and ultimately improved. With the right system and feedback, you can train your brain to handle challenges better.

Clear Definitions and Developmental Framing

What Is Mental Toughness?

There are many definitions of mental toughness. Psychologists, coaches, counselors, and entrepreneurs all look at the concept from different angles. However, they all agree on one thing: mental toughness is *not* about being emotionless or "perfect." It's about being adaptable under stress, whether it's about motivation, pressure, or concentration.

A mentally tough person can stay focused when distractions hit. They manage their emotions instead of being ruled by them. They believe in their ability to respond to different situations, not just impulsively react. Finally, they can make clear decisions, even if outcomes appear uncertain.

In short, mental toughness is a mixture of:

- Attention control
- Emotional regulation
- Adaptive confidence
- Decision resilience

Other definitions of mental toughness include looking at it through a timeline of competition:

- Setting your goals (before a competition)
- Coping with the pressures of a game (during a competition)
- Dealing with mistakes and/or losing (after a competition)

These three factors can also serve as an excellent guide to what mental toughness is.

Plus, the 4C model of mental toughness is another excellent way of defining and clarifying it into distinct chunks:

- Control (not allowing outside forces to control you, but the other way around)
- Commitment (not giving up, no matter what)
- Challenge (difficulties are lessons, not obstacles)
- Confidence (believing in yourself and your abilities)

All this can seem overwhelming, like there's a lot expected of you. However, Rome wasn't built in a day, and neither will your mindset. The following chapters will take you through each facet of mental toughness, one by one, clarifying and providing direct skills and practices to help develop it.

Psychologist Albert Bandura introduced the concept of **self-efficacy**, which will be a primary factor throughout this book. It is the belief that you can take any action to achieve a goal, even under pressure. When you have high self-efficacy, you trust yourself to handle what comes your way, which fuels your confidence and leads to *action*.

What Mental Toughness Is *Not*

It's important to remember that toughness isn't about never failing. You will be introduced to the concept of the growth mindset, which emphasizes that real toughness means staying engaged when things are up in the air. This involves *learning* from failure instead of being crushed by it. You're not defined by one bad game or one fumble.

You're defined by how you respond.

- *It's not aggression.* Acting out of frustration or anger doesn't make you strong.
- *It's not stoicism.* Ignoring or hiding your emotions will only backfire later.

- ***It's not forced grit.*** Pushing past your limits without rest will lead to burnout.

True toughness is flexible. It relies on understanding long-term goals and motivation, always looking to the future rather than getting stuck in a single moment. One of the ways you'll learn to do this is through **Self-Determination Theory**:

- *Autonomy:* feeling like you have choice and ownership.
- *Competence:* seeing your skills grow through feedback.
- *Relatedness:* being supported by others while you grow.

When your training and environment support these needs, mental toughness becomes something you want to build rather than something you're forced to fake. Remember the word "environment," because toughness grows through interaction with your surroundings and constraints. Growth happens *in context*, in games, classrooms, conversations, and mistakes, *not* in isolation.

That is why this book is focused on you, young adult athletes. Your context is different. Your abilities and mental capacities have started to grow and mature, and so you've entered a new developmental stage. For younger kids aged around eight to twelve, they need more concrete techniques, ones where toughness is built through game-like challenges and fun tasks with immediate feedback and encouragement.

For teens and young adults like you, toughness is developed through more reflection, self-assessment, and peer modeling. The techniques aren't just given to you as direct orders; what you need is to work your mind by observing your teammates, analyzing your reactions, and setting your own goals.

Core Pillars to Be Trained (The Book's Map)

This book isn't just going to throw vague and abstract concepts at you; it's going to break everything down into observable and trainable pillars. Each comes with a one-line spoken cue for coaches and parents to use as signals for your mind to "snap back" into the necessary mindset.

These are the building blocks of all the chapters to come:

1. *Focus*

Focus means keeping your attention on what matters and refocusing whenever your mind drifts (which is expected). This process is what creates "flow," that feeling of total absorption in what you're doing. When you're in flow, time disappears, and your best performance can feel effortless.

The best way to measure this is by evaluating your ability and the time it takes you to recover your attention after distractions.

Coach Cue: *"Bring your focus back now."*

2. *Emotion Regulation*

Pressure isn't going to disappear. School, friends, chores, responsibilities—these are constants in our lives and impossible to ignore. You just need to learn how to handle them. Emotional regulation is your ability to stay composed when stress hits.

Breathing routines, reset rituals, and positive self-talk are practical tools for this, and they help you observe just how quickly you bounce back from mistakes and frustration.

Coach Cue: *"Breathe, reset, play."*

3. *Confidence and Identity*

You're not going to pretend like nothing bothers you or that you can do everything perfectly. You're going to *believe* that you can figure things out. Confidence is rooted in self-efficacy: *"I can do this."* Over time, this belief shapes your identity: how you see yourself in your role, your sport, and your passion.

Start noting how many times you choose to be challenged rather than stay in your comfort zone. That shows that you're confident and secure enough in your abilities.

Coach Cue: *"You've done this before."*

4.   Decision Intelligence

This is the ability to make wise choices under uncertain circumstances, to act decisively when there's no perfect option. With this pillar, it's practically integrating focus, confidence, and emotion regulation into *action*.

Measure it by how fast and effectively you respond in dynamic situations.

Coach Cue: *"Scan, decide, act."*

Together, these four pillars form your mental toughness blueprint. They're the cogs and gears, fitting and running together smoothly to make the machinery of your mind and body work. Strengthen one, and the others grow as well.

You don't need to embody all four pillars every day and at every stage of your athletic journey. Their emphasis and importance shift constantly, and it is another sign of mental toughness to be able to adjust each pillar according to your role and the season:

- **Early season:** Focus and confidence matter most as you set goals and rebuild your rhythm.
- **Midseason:** Decision-making and emotional regulation become increasingly important as pressure mounts.

- **Late season:** Integrating all together matters. Your routines, recovery, and composure under fatigue make the difference.

Each phase teaches and instills something new. You don't have to master everything at once. Just train for what the moment demands.

Ethics and Safety

Mental toughness training is about growth, not grind.

It's not about ignoring pain, overworking, or bottling emotions. If training your mind ever feels like a battle you're losing every day, something needs to change. If you notice any of these warning signs on your journey, then it's time to pause, take a step back, and reevaluate:

- Sleep loss
- Mood swings
- Burnout
- Academic decline

As Matthew Walker shows in *Why We Sleep*, mental and physical recovery depend on proper rest. Without it, your brain can't learn, adapt, or manage stress effectively. A tough mindset doesn't mean pushing through exhaustion. If it's tearing you apart to do things, then that is no longer your best. Recovery in itself *is* part of the work.

There are plenty of ways you can communicate with your body and track your levels and progress. Biofeedback and journaling tools, such as heart rate monitors or focus apps, are handy. However, these are *aids*, not definitions of your worth. Getting bogged down in the numbers and feeling like a "failure" if you don't meet specific criteria does no one any good. You need to use these tools wisely and only with adult and professional guidance.

Mental toughness must grow in an environment of trust, transparency, and support—and that includes with yourself as well.

1. You should always feel safe expressing emotions without judgment, even going to a mental health professional, should you need or want to.
2. Parents and coaches should be included in your process, yes, but *not* to control it. Their job is to understand and guide you in *your* capacity and goals, as opposed to what *they* expect or think you should be capable of.
3. Conversations about your performance, fears, and anxieties must remain confidential (between you and your coach or between you and your parents). They are not entitled to speak about you to others, while you must be respectful of their guidance and authority, so long as they respect your autonomy and control over your own life.

If you ever feel pressured to "rough it out" in ways that harm your well-being, understand that this is not strength. That's neglect.

Proper motivation and toughness come from choice. That means your journey should never feel like someone else's checklist. When it comes from the inside, from wanting to improve or compete, you become unstoppable. Coaches and parents are there to empower, not dictate.

You are the one behind the wheel.

Measurement, Baselines, and Micro Metrics

When people hear "measurement," they often think of high-tech tools, like fitness watches, data dashboards, or apps that track every heartbeat and second of sleep. However, when you're just starting to understand your mental game, you don't need all that fancy stuff. The best baseline tools are the simplest ones, the ones you can actually use every day.

A **baseline** means your starting point. It's the snapshot of how you're currently performing, not in stats or scores, but in reflective ideas like the pillars before. Once you know your baseline, you can track how much you grow over time.

The following checklists and exercises aren't meant to highlight your "faults." They're areas of improvement. You can review them once a week or before a new season to track your progress and highlight areas for growth. Once you've recognized which area needs the most attention right now, you can be selective about which exercises and practices you can do to improve.

The One-Page Checklist

Focus: *"How well do I stay locked in?"*

	Rarely	Sometimes	Often	Almost Always
I listen and pay attention when my coach gives directions.	☐	☐	☐	☐
I can get my focus back quickly after something goes wrong.	☐	☐	☐	☐
I notice what's happening in the game (my position, timing, teammates).	☐	☐	☐	☐

Arousal: *"How well do I manage my energy?"*

	Rarely	Sometimes	Often	Almost Always
I feel ready and alert when practice or games start.	☐	☐	☐	☐
I can calm myself down or fire myself up when needed.	☐	☐	☐	☐
I stay composed under pressure or during mistakes.	☐	☐	☐	☐

Confidence: *"How much do I believe in myself?"*

	Rarely	Sometimes	Often	Almost Always
I bounce back fast when I mess up.	☐	☐	☐	☐
I use positive self-talk (like "I got this," or "Bring it on!")	☐	☐	☐	☐
I take feedback well and don't let it crush my confidence.	☐	☐	☐	☐

The 60-Second Self-Rating

Sometimes, there isn't enough time to carefully go through a whole checklist, whether it's right before practice or a competition. That's why you can take 30 to 60 seconds and use this check-in:

How focused am I right now?

1	2	3	4	5

How ready am I to give my best effort?

1	2	3	4	5

How confident am I feeling?

1	2	3	4	5

No overthinking, no judgment- no one else needs to see this. Just circle your number. You're not aiming for a perfect "5" every time (which would be virtually impossible). Some days you'll feel like a "2" across the board. That's fine. It's about knowing what you can accommodate that day and how you can still practice and play within your own parameters. Plus, you'll start noticing trends.

Maybe you're less focused when you have an exam that morning, or you feel more ready after a filling meal or a good night's sleep. This will help you understand your mind and work around it. And when you see the rating move up over a few weeks, you'll feel that progress.

The Coach Observation Sheet

Athlete Name: _____

Coach: _____

Session Type: ☐ Practice ☐ Game ☐ Scrimmage

Session Type	Positive Body Language (1-5)	Engagement (1-5)	Consistency (1-5)	Observable Behaviors

Coaches can also track key behaviors per session (which remain the same across a particular run). These should be parameters that aren't necessarily physical skills, but ones that reveal your mindset.

For instance:

- Body language can be observed, particularly after mistakes (slumped shoulders vs. quick reset).
- Engagement during drills (active participation vs. zoning out).

- Effort consistency (steady intensity vs. giving up early).

The most powerful confidence booster isn't someone telling you, "You're great" or "You did well today." It's seeing proof, no matter how minuscule, that you do have control.

Micro Metrics and Small Wins

Once your baseline is clear, it's time to measure progress, even if not in giant leaps. One of the best ways to track mental toughness is through **micro metrics**: small, frequent indicators of improvement that keep you aware.

For example:

- How long does it take you to bounce back after a mistake?
- How many minutes can you stay entirely focused before drifting?
- Whether you recorded your nightly reflection or skipped it.

Angela Duckworth, who wrote *Grit: The Power of Passion and Perseverance*, showed that real toughness comes from tracking small wins over long stretches of time. Big goals are inspiring, but they're also easy to quit on because progress feels slow. The fact of the matter is, most people overestimate what they can do in a day (wanting to fill up their days with large tasks that they couldn't possibly achieve). This often leads to disappointment and being disheartened. However, people *underestimate* what they can do in a year (by taking small cumulative steps over a longer stretch of time). Metrics give you those steps as something to celebrate every day.

Maybe your bounce-back time dropped from 60 seconds to 45. That's a win! Or you kept a focus streak for five straight practices. Another win! These small victories are the building blocks of toughness. This way, you focus on the proof that effort adds up instead of just the outcomes.

Instead of thinking, "Did I win?" ask, "Did I improve my process today, no matter how small?" That subtle shift matters.

Visual Progress = Motivation

Visual tools often turn invisible progress into something you can *see*. These could be streak calendars in apps or physically, bar charts or graphs your coach could put together showing timestamps and other parameters that can be quantitatively measured, or even progress walls and journals.

The purpose of these is also to maintain consistency as **frequency beats duration**. Daily 2-minute logs create more substantial behavioral change than a once-a-month reflection because they rewire your habits. Tracking these small wins creates **feedback loops**- real-time signals that tell your brain, "You're getting better."

The more you see progress, the more you'll want to keep going.

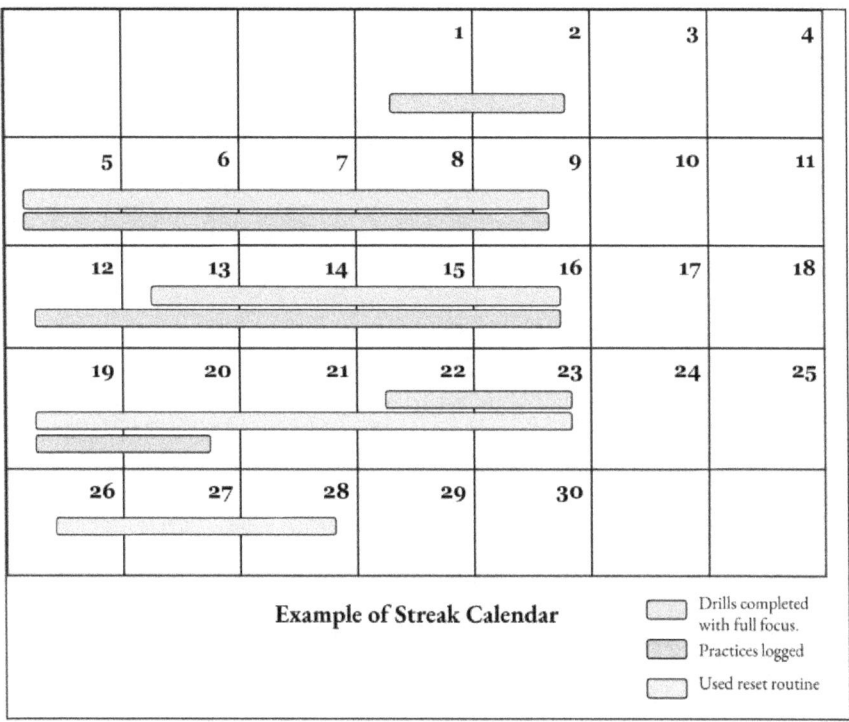

Iteration Cycle for Programs

Now that you know how to measure small things, it's time to use that data to improve. Growth doesn't happen in one straight line, but in a loop. This is called an **iteration cycle**: a way to keep refining your approach instead of just repeating the same thing and hoping for better results.

For young athletes, this cycle can take the form of:

Test → Micro-experiment → Review → Adapt

Step 1: Test

Pick one key skill or mental habit to measure.

Write down the baseline for this skill (perhaps using your checklist, self-rating, or coach observation).

Example: "I usually lose focus after a mistake. Rated my focus 2/5 in the last three practices."

Step 2: Micro-Experiment

Spend two weeks (10 to 14 days, or around 6 to 10 practices) trying one small but deliberate change. The key is to choose just *one variable* to adjust, like:

- Doing a 1-minute breathing reset before drills.
- Using a "next play" cue word after mistakes.
- Tracking hydration and sleep before training sessions.

Keep everything else consistent.

Example: "For two weeks, I'll take three deep breaths to reset every time I make a mistake."

Step 3: Review

Retest yourself using the same tools from Step 1. Compare the ratings and observations side by side. This includes your focus, energy, and confidence; your performance metric; and any qualitative notes, such as how you felt and your consistency.

Ask reflection questions:

- "Did my focus improve?"
- "Did it feel natural or forced?"

Example: "My focus ratings went from 2/5 to 4/5. Breathing felt easy after a few days. Helped me bounce back faster."

Step 4: Adapt

Here is where you turn your learning into your next action plan.

If it worked, make it part of your pre-practice or in-game routine. Then, move on to a different skill and start Step 1 again.

If it was only partly effective, tweak the timing or frequency, and figure out how to adjust it.

If no change happened, replace it and try a new micro-experiment. And it's back to Step 1!

Example: "Keep the breathing reset, but add a focus cue word before drills. Next micro-experiment: test 'next play' cues."

Within these micro-experiments, you can try multiple things. For example, if you practice a team sport or train with others, you can use what's called an "A/B approach." Here, each group tries a different idea to tackle the skill, and then you compare the results.

- **Group A**: Uses the "reset" breath technique.
- **Group B**: Uses a positive self-talk technique.

Furthermore, during the Adapt step, you (or your coach) can set your own decision rules. This means that there are pre-defined thresholds for what you will do once the results are in:

- Continue if engagement/focus/energy increased by 20% or more.
- Modify if results were inconsistent.
- Stop if stress or frustration levels rise.

The goal isn't to "win" the experiment. The goal is to learn what works best for you.

Novel Framing: Mental Skills as Micro-Habits

Beyond deliberate experimentation with micro-metrics, mental toughness also benefits from **micro-dosing mental practice**. Think of it as consistent mind reps that you can fit into the small cracks of your day, two to five minutes of focused mental work before or after practice that adds up to growth over time.

In *Foundations of Sport and Exercise Psychology*, Weinberg and Gould describe how short bouts of mental training sessions enhance focus, confidence, and performance. The key is **intentionality**: being fully present for a few minutes rather than half-distracted for an hour.

Some drills:

- **Pre-Practice Visualization:** Before you even touch your gear or step onto a court, take three minutes to visualize yourself performing your drills with control. Picture the sounds, the feeling of movement, the rhythm of your breath. Visualization activates the same neural pathways as actual movement, so think of it as a rehearsal.

- **Post-Drill Reset Breathing**: After each drill or rep, take one deep breath in, one slow exhale out, and mentally label what went well. This teaches your brain to reset between actions, rather than carry tension or frustration into the next play.

- **Nightly Reflection**: Before bed, write down one moment in your day when you felt focused, even if it was small. This shifts your attention from mistakes to progress, wiring your brain for growth.

To make these drills even easier to remember, use **habit anchoring**: linking new mental reps to existing actions you already do automatically.

For example:

- Visualize success while tying your shoes.
- Do reset breathing during a water break.

- Reflect on focus while cooling down and stretching.

This trick turns self-discipline into routine. Over time, your mental micro-habits should go through three stages: the **Progression Model.**

1. **Frequency:** Start with daily reps, even if they're little.
2. **Duration:** Gradually lengthen your mental practice from two minutes to five, then ten.
3. **Complexity:** Once you're consistent, add more advanced drills, such as emotional labeling or game-situation visualizations.

Team and Household Alignment

Mental toughness cannot grow in isolation. Your systems, like your team, coaches, and family, all need to communicate. You could be the most disciplined athlete in the world, but if your environment is chaotic or discouraging, your progress will stall.

Start by creating a **Team Mental Mission**: one sentence that defines your group's shared values. Something like:

"We have the same mission but different roles: to build a strong mind through sport."

Once that shared mission becomes clear, you can use these three levers to solidify it:

1. **Routines**: Set consistent times for mental check-ins. Maybe your team starts every practice with one minute of breathing or ends with one reflection question. Repetition makes mindset work automatic.
2. **Rituals**: Create moments that hold emotional weight, like a team huddle or a focus circle with your coach before games. Rituals transform mental skills from theory to identity.

3. **Reinforcement**: Most teams celebrate wins, but *great* teams will also celebrate effort and bounce-back. When you reward players for responding well to mistakes instead of just results, you shape lasting behavior.

This doesn't only apply to teams but also to households. Parents and coaches play a key role in reinforcing the right kind of mental toughness.

Parent/Coach Pact

> *We agree that every athlete's growth, mental, emotional, and physical, depends on the environment we create together.*
>
> *Coaches coach.*
>
> *Parents support.*
>
> *Players learn.*
>
> *We are one team with one mindset.*

Coach Scripts:

- **At the start of the season:** "My goal isn't just to build athletes, but to help your kids build strong minds."
- **After challenging games:** "This is all part of their growth curve. We'll review and get better."
- **When parents ask about playing time:** "We're coaching the process, not just the minutes. Improvement will earn opportunities."

Parent Scripts:

- **Before practices and games:** "Have fun and play hard!"

- **After a win:** "I loved watching you play. You looked focused and confident."
- **After a loss:** "Tough games teach the biggest lessons. I'm proud of how you handled it.

When coaches and parents align their words and expectations, athletes feel safer to experiment, fail, and grow.

Alignment might be:

- **Team Routine:** Start every practice with a focus cue.
- **Coach Ritual:** Celebrate composure moments after games, not just the scoreboard.
- **Parent Reinforcement:** Ask about effort and mindset, not just stats.

Low-Friction Toolkits

Portable and easy-to-use tools for mental fitness practice.

Pocket Cards: Perfect for taping to clipboards or sticking in gym bags.

Reset Card

Take three breaths.
Feel your feet against the ground.
Recommit to your effort.

Focus Cue

Forget the last play.
Fully focus on what's next.

Confidence Card

Remember one rep or drill you nailed this week.

Calm under pressure

Pressure is proof you care.
Channel it.

> **Growth Cue**
> Win or lose, what did today teach you?.

Micro-Journals: These take under two minutes a day, but provide a powerful reflection tool.

Date: _____

1. What went well today?
2. One thing I'm improving:
3. One mindset skill I practiced (focus, calm, confidence, etc.):
4. My next challenge:
5. One thing I'm grateful for:

Printable Flashcards: For younger athletes, cards with emotional regulation prompts can be beneficial.

Front	Back
Missed a goal/point.	Reset, Refocus, Re-engage.
Coach gave difficult feedback.	Listen, learn, and adjust.
Teammate messed up.	Encourage, don't blame.
Feeling nervous.	Nerves are readiness energy.
You're losing.	Keep your standards high and focus on effort first and foremost.

Coach Timers: Use short timers during practice for quick "mental breaks."

2-minute Reset – Mid-practice

"Find your breath. Eyes up. Three deep inhales, three slow exhales. Visualize your next rep done right."

60-second Reflection – After drills or scrimmages

"What worked? What needs a tweak?"

3-minute Rehearsal – Pre-game

"You're down points near the end of the game. See it. Trust your routine. What do you do?"

Cue Library: A collection of shared vocabulary that can be used as verbal anchors during practice.

"Next play."	"Steady breath."	"Trust your work."
"Eyes up."	"Relax shoulders."	"Strong and steady."
"Lock in."	"Find your rhythm."	"Go all in."
"One thing at a time."	"Effort before outcome."	"Own it."
"Find your anchor."	"Patience yields focus."	"Calm and control."

To launch these tools successfully, try running a 20-minute onboarding session for your team or group. Keep it fun and collaborative:

- **Introduce the Four Pillars:** Focus, Emotion, Confidence, and Decision-Making.

- **Explain the Why**: Solidify your group's shared mission and the purpose for you all being here.

- **Hand Out Tools**: Figure out which ones you want to use, explain them, or hand them out (pocket cards and flashcards).

- **Set Shared Goals**: Agree on one mental habit to practice daily for the next month.

This session builds immediate buy-in when people see the tools in front of them and understand the "why," they're more likely to cooperate and use them consistently.

As Weinberg and Gould remind us, the science of sport psychology only creates results when it's translated into action. Reading theories is all well and good, but you also need to apply small, repeatable behaviors that actually create mental strength. When you treat mental toughness like physical skills, something to be trained daily, tracked consistently, and supported by your environment, progress becomes inevitable.

When you turn the page to the next chapter, you begin breaking down the pillars of mental toughness, starting with how athletes hone their focus and attention through pre-performance routines, attention states, and constraint-led games.

Key Takeaways

- Mental toughness relies on four core pillars: Attention Control, Emotion Regulation, Adaptive Confidence, and Decision Intelligence.

- It is vital to understand your baseline levels of each pillar, measure them frequently with micro-metrics, and consistently adapt them through iteration cycles.

- All parts of an athlete's network (player, team, parents, coaches) should be aligned around a shared mental mission to promote cognitive skills alongside physical ones, turning them into micro-habits.

Champion Mantra:

"Mental toughness is not born; it is designed."

Chapter 2: Focus and Attention

The athlete who controls attention controls the outcome.

What does that mean?

Every play, every shot, every decision in sport happens in the span of a few seconds. In those seconds, athletes have to lock in, blocking out distractions, fear, and overthinking. Focus is the first pillar that will hold up your mental toughness game. Losing concentration at times and distractions are inevitable. However, if you can find your focus fast, hold it under pressure, and recover it when it slips, you can rise to any occasion.

Mastering attention involves entering a state psychologist Mihaly Csikszentmihalyi called **flow:** that zone where time disappears, your movements feel automatic, and everything clicks. Flow isn't random, and it isn't innate. It's built through deliberate attention training that we'll explore in this chapter.

Attention States and Development

Focus grows just like muscle strength, and the size of your "attention window" depends partly on your age and training history. A 9-year-old might stay intensely focused for 10 to 15 minutes before their mind drifts, while a 16-year-old athlete who's been training for years can hold their attention for 30 minutes or more, especially in a challenging, game-like environment.

Typical Attention Spans for Athletes:

- *Ages 8 – 11*: ten to fifteen minutes of full engagement per task.

  $10:00$ — $15:00$

- *Ages 12 – 15*: fifteen to twenty-five minutes, with increasing ability to refocus after breaks.

  $15:00$ — $25:00$

- *Ages 16+ and advanced*: twenty-five to forty minutes of sustained concentration, especially with structured goals or game simulation.

  $25:00$ — $40:00$

That means a '90-minute practice' doesn't mean *90 minutes of solid focus*. Brilliant coaches plan around attention rhythms by having short, intense blocks with built-in resets.

For younger kids, the goal is training focus through play. Use varied drills that demand quick reactions, such as tag, balance games, or mini challenges lasting under five minutes. These activities develop what's called **selective attention**: the skill of locking onto the task that matters and ignoring the rest.

For teens, the training begins to shift to **metacognitive focus**: thinking about your own thinking.

This includes noticing:

- *"When does my focus drop?"*
- *"What triggers it? Boredom, frustration, or distraction?"*
- *"How do I bring it back fast?"*

This awareness is your gateway to flow. Csikszentmihalyi showed that athletes reach flow when challenges perfectly match their skills- so not too easy, not too hard. You can create that balance yourself by setting micro-goals at each drill: *"I'll stay focused for three consecutive reps,"* or *"I'll reset with a deep breath after every miss."*

Finally, attention needs also vary between multi-sport and single-sport athletes. Multi-sport athletes often have broader attention adaptability. Meaning they can switch between tasks more quickly and respond to complex environments. Single-sport athletes might develop a deep, narrow focus, which is ideal for precision roles. Both paths are valuable, but what matters is learning to shift between narrow and broad attention when the moment calls for it.

Mapping Attention States to Sport Roles

Every sport has its own "attention fingerprint." Some roles require **laser focus** (tuning out everything except one small target), while others demand **panoramic awareness** (reading the whole field at once). Knowing your natural focus type and what your position in the sport requires will help you train smarter.

Examples of Narrow Focus Roles:

- Basketball shooters before release
- Soccer strikers on a finishing touch
- A golfer reading a putt

These athletes thrive in what psychologists call a **closed-skill environment**: predictable, repetitive movements that rely on precision and timing. The challenge is blocking out internal noise (like self-doubt) and staying tuned to cues (like the ball's spin).

Examples of Broad Attention Roles:

- Quarterback scanning receivers
- Goalkeeper reading opponents
- Point guard orchestrating plays

These roles operate in **open-skill environments** that are unpredictable and fast-changing. Here, you must process multiple cues simultaneously and adapt in real time.

Most elite athletes can switch between these states on command. This skill is known as **attentional flexibility**. You can train it through constraints-led practice, a method explored by Davids, Button, and Bennett in their *Dynamics of Skill Acquisition*. Instead of repeating drills the same way, you tweak the 'constraints' (the rules, the environment, the task, the limitations) to force the brain to adapt its attention style.

"...the emphasis during learning should be on encouraging change and adaptation rather than achieving some hypothetical idealized state."

(Davids, Button, & Bennett, 2008, p.96)

Example Drills for Mid-Play Switching:

- ***Color Call Drill (Soccer)***: Coach shouts a color mid-dribble. The player must pass the ball instantly to the matching cone. This forces a broad-to-narrow shift.

- ***Reaction Mirror (Basketball)***: Partner moves side-to-side unpredictably. Your goal is to mirror without guessing. Builds awareness and anticipation.

- ***Countdown Cue (Any Sport)***: Have a teammate randomly call "focus!" mid-play. Take one breath and immediately narrow your attention to the most relevant cue (for example, your target).

Extra Habit:

Tag your focus state before drills. Say out loud, "Narrow focus" or "Broad view." It's a quick mental switch that primes your brain for the correct mode. Over time, it becomes automatic. Your mind will know how to find the right focus state on demand.

Measurement and Micro-Benchmarks

Focus might seem like something invisible, but you can measure and track it like strength or speed. Consistent tracking keeps you accountable and helps you notice improvement.

Focus Streak Counter:

With each practice or scrimmage, note how many complete plays you execute with full focus, with no mental breaks and no self-talk spiral. When your attention slips, restart the counter. You can use tracking apps, a bullet journal, mark a physical sheet, or use post-its on a wall or board.

Example:

Week 1: Maximum 3-play streak before distraction.

Day 1											
Day 2											
Day 3											

Day 4											
Day 5											

Week 3: Maximum 7-play streak before distraction.

Day 1											
Day 2											
Day 3											
Day 4											
Day 5											

Week 5: Achieved 10+ plays with sustained focus.

Day 1											
Day 2											
Day 3											
Day 4											

Day 5										

Here's a blank 7-day template you could use to track your own weekly streak. You could even add qualitative, reflective notes next to each day, noting what distracted you or how you felt that day, to detect patterns in what tends to break your focus.

Day 1										
Day 2										
Day 3										
Day 4										
Day 5										
Day 6										
Day 7										

Coach 'Snap Check' Method:

This is a quick observational tool for coaches, but you can also use it for self-assessment. Every few minutes, a coach (or teammate) watches your body language and reactions for three seconds:

- *Eyes*. Are they locked on relevant cues?

- **Body**. Balanced or fidgeting?
- **Response Time**. Smooth or delayed?

These observations create a focus pulse, or real-time feedback loop.

Weekly Review:

Once a week, review your attention data, including your focus streaks (as quantitative information), your personal notes (the qualitative bits), and your coach and/or teammates' feedback.

Then, compare it to the baseline that you've determined in the previous chapter. Celebrate all progress, even small wins. When you notice improvement, link it back to your systems and environment: What helped you stay focused longer this week? Or which environmental factors may have led to less focus? Maybe you slept better, or the drills were shorter. Perhaps you had a challenging exam that day or a personal situation. By experimenting and understanding these "constraints," you're following the exact process used by elite athletes. That's how flow stability develops.

Practical Routines and Auto-Triggers

Entrance Rituals That Work

All athletes, regardless of sport, need a getaway or a simple, reliable "trick" to flip the switch from everyday life to competition mode. This is what we call an **entrance ritual**. It's not superstition or luck, but a psychological focusing technique. Once done consistently, entrance rituals can train your brain to associate specific actions with a state of readiness. Think of it like pressing 'play' on your flow state. By recognizing a familiar sequence, this state is triggered.

Three-Step Pre-Play Routine:

1. **Breath**: Begin with one deep and slow inhale through your nose, then exhale through your mouth. This calms your nervous system and centers your attention.

   Example: A soccer player standing before kickoff takes one calm breath, drops their shoulders, and locks eyes on the field.

2. ***Cue Word***: A single word that captures your mindset. Choose something short, powerful, and personal. This acts as a verbal trigger.

Example: A basketball player whispers "Sharp" before stepping onto the court to remind themselves to stay alert.

3. ***Visual Micro-Script***: A brief mental image of your first successful action. This could be driving the ball, making a solid first serve, or landing a clean jump. The goal is to program and prime your motor system to fire correctly under pressure.

Templates By Sport or Role:

To create your own 3-step pre-play routine, first think of how many breaths you need to take to reset your body and center your focus. At this stage, which body parts could you bring attention to that would help?

Then get into the trigger mindset and choose one or two words that match your role/position.

Finally, mentally rehearse your first five seconds.

Below are some examples of rituals in different sports and roles. Use them as launchpads to formulate your own.

Team Sports	
Soccer: Midfielder - **Breath:** Two deep breaths through the nose, one long exhale. - **Cue Word:** "Control" - **Visual Micro-Script:** See yourself receiving the ball clearly, scanning upfield, threading a clever pass.	**Basketball: Shooter** - Inhale for 3, exhale for 3. - "Locked in" - See the ball arc perfectly, swish through the net. Smooth form, relaxed hands.
Hockey: Goalie - Inhale through the nose, exhale through the mouth. - "Command" - See the puck moving in slow motion. Your glove snaps it away.	**Volleyball: Server** - One slow breath while spinning the ball. - "Own it." - See the serve floating just above the net, landing hard where you aimed.

Water Polo: Player	Football: Quarterback
- Two slow inhales through the nose, one long exhale through the mouth. - "Strong" - Picture the first few seconds of play, the lane opening, your position perfect, a clean pass to a teammate	- 2 deep breaths, one steady exhale. - "Lead" - See the play unfold, with protection holding, your throw sharp, receiver in stride.

Individual Sports

Track: Sprinter	Swimming: Swimmer
- 3 short inhales, one long exhale through the mouth. - "Calm" - See the first three strides as rhythmic and clean, with no	- Deep belly inhale, slow exhale. - "Flow" - See yourself slicing through the water, first strokes perfect, body gliding firmly.

rushing.	
Boxing/Martial Arts: Fighter - 4-count inhale, 2-count hold, 4-count exhale. - "Center" - See yourself reading your opponent, every movement clear. You're fluid, balanced, untouchable.	**Gymnastics: Gymnast** - 4-count inhale, 4-count exhale. - "Grace" - Imagine your exact start with a salute, deep breath, and your first skill clean and confident.

Precision Roles

Tennis: Player - Inhale through the nose, exhale while bouncing the ball. - "Laser focus" - See your serve landing exactly in your target zone. Smooth contact	**Baseball: Pitcher** - Exhale longer than inhale - "Precision." - See the strike zone. Picture the pitch slicing through it, exactly where you want it.

and follow-through.	

No two athletes' rituals are identical, but they all serve the same purpose: stabilizing focus and preparing your body for an automatic performance.

To get the most out of the ritual, repeat it every day, even outside of practice. This is a **habituation strategy**, which combines **daily repetition** with **varied contexts**. Tie the ritual to warm-ups, training, exams, and school presentations. Then, change your environment. Do it in noisy settings, after mistakes, or even when you're tired. By constantly practicing under different conditions, your brain learns to trigger focus even when things don't feel perfect. Over time, your entrance ritual becomes a reliable gateway into flow, no matter the situation.

In-Play Micro-Cues

Once you're in the game, attention can still wander. Distractions, mistakes, and pressure pile on. That's why you also need cues to recenter mid-action. These are anchors that snap your attention back to what matters most in the moment: the next play.

Cues like this work because they connect physical sensations with mental focus.

One-Word Triggers:

Short, but high-impact words that refocus your attention.

- *"Now."*
- *"Calm."*
- *"Push."*

- *"Locked."*
- *"Look."*
- *"Up."*
- *"Power."*
- *"Charge."*

Tactile Anchors:

A physical action that reconnects your mind and body.

- Wiping your hands on a towel.
- Tapping your leg.
- Adjusting your wristband.
- Tapping equipment (for example, a tennis racket).
- Quickly wiping palms on the uniform.
- Reset grip (for ball, bat, putt, or racket).

Rhythm Breath:

One smooth inhale-exhale sequence to calm your system between plays or points. It's a tiny break that restores mental clarity without losing intensity.

The trick is that you can't expect these cues to work in high-pressure situations if you only ever try them in games. They must be built into your daily training until they become reflexes. During drills, consciously pair your micro-cues with key actions.

For example:

- After every mistake, exhale and whisper your one-word trigger.

- Before every serve or kickoff, do your tactile anchor (touch your wristband).
- In between drills, regain your rhythmic breath.

Eventually, your brain links these actions to focus and recovery. That's **automaticity:** a principle drawn from motor learning research and supported by Davids et al. (2008). Repetition under varying constraints makes skills adaptive, not robotic.

You don't do all of this in isolation. Coaches play a significant role in reinforcing these habits.

The best prompting follows three simple rules:

1. *Frequency*: Only occasional reminders and cues. Over-coaching can break focus.
2. *Tone*: Keep it calm, consistent, and neutral. It's a reminder, not a correction.
3. *Timing*: After breaks or between reps, not mid-action.

Remember, Coach: We want the athlete to build self-directed focus rather than depend on external commands. If you see your athlete self-correct or remind themselves of the cue, then take a step back.

The 10-Second Reset Protocol

Every athlete makes mistakes. So, you need to work around resetting after them (because it's impossible to avoid them entirely). The key is to recover without losing momentum due to interruptions or frustration.

Step 1: Physical Micro-Reset (Body First)

When annoyance hits, your body often tightens. Shoulders tense, breathing shortens, and movements become jerky. The first step is to release that tension physically.

- Drop your shoulders.
- Loosen your stance.
- Shake out your hands and legs.

Step 2: Single Breath (Control the System)

Take one deliberate inhale through your nose and exhale through your mouth. Focus entirely on that breath.

Step 3: Target Cue Word (Direct Attention Forward)

Choose a cue word that shifts your focus to the next play or goal.

- *"Next."*
- *"Don't mind."*
- *"Forward."*
- *"One more."*

Use this technique after a missed shot, turnover, or foul. Reset during timeouts or referee interruptions. You can even do it after a teammate makes a mistake that pulls your focus away (this will not only help you refocus, but will also keep your frustrations in check so they're not taken out on your teammate).

When you use this protocol effectively and noticeably bounce back fast from situations, your coach, teammates, and even you should acknowledge it. Reinforcement after success creates positive feedback loops that help solidify this ritual and have it become instinctive.

Creative Training: Games, Constraints, and Tech

Constraint-Led Attention Games

As you've seen, one of the best ways to train focus is to push your attention to the limit and watch it adapt. This is where the **constraints-led approach** comes in. As explained by Davids, Button, and Bennett

(2008), athletes grow fastest when their environment shapes their behavior instead of being told exactly what to do.

Your brain learns best when the situation itself forces you to figure things out.

Imagine a soccer game where the field is smaller, the teams are uneven, or the ball changes color mid-play. Suddenly, you can't rely on autopilot. You have to *notice* what's happening. These are constraint-led attention games: creative games that tweak the rules or conditions, forcing players to read new clues and adapt constantly.

Start simple. For example, in basketball, play a 3v3 on a half-court where each team can only pass with their non-dominant hand. The constraint automatically narrows your focus and prevents you from falling back on habit.

Then, you might rotate the cue condition: one round where you can only score after three passes, another where a coach yells out a color, and you must pass the ball to the area of the court where the colored cone is. Every change forces your brain to tune in differently.

Next, you layer **progression**. As players improve, the environment becomes noisier and less predictable. Add music, crown sounds, or random cues to simulate distractions. You can even try low-visibility games (like wearing tinted goggles or playing in dim light) to train your eyes and brain to work together more effectively. Or shift the rules mid-game without warning, pushing players to update their focus in real time.

The goal isn't to "win" these games, but to strengthen attention flexibility. You're building the skill of switching focus efficiently, something top athletes do instinctively in high-pressure moments.

To measure if this training transfers to real performance, track the play metrics:

- Reaction time after a cue or whistle
- Pass accuracy under noise
- Mistakes per possession when visibility drops
- Focus on "losses" (times when you freeze, look away, or hesitate).

Keep short notes after each session. After a few weeks, you'll notice patterns, like your reaction time shortening, your decisions becoming sharper, and your eyes moving more deliberately.

Tokenized Focus Economy

Sometimes, consistency needs a little bit of motivation. Focus is a fickle thing, and it drifts, especially when training gets repetitive. That's why we need to try to make focus *itself* rewarding.

Team Focus Tokens

This is an excellent option for team sports. Along with your coach, you create a shared system of 'focus tokens.' These could be anything from marbles to cards to just points noted down by the coach. You earn them for specific, measurable blocks of sustained attention, such as ten minutes of uninterrupted drill work or a full scrimmage without a single distraction.

At the end of the week, these tokens can be redeemed for privileges. Maybe early access to a gear, a say in the next practice game, or music choice during warm-up. The rewards don't have to be big. This system trains focus under accountability and teamwork built on attention, connecting team focus with shared progress. Everyone wants the group to stay sharp because collective focus means collective gain. It's a social version of self-regulation.

However, Deci and Ryan's *Self-Determination Theory* (2000) helps us understand a hiccup. If you rely too heavily on external rewards, motivation can fade. You start performing for the *reward* instead of focusing on the skill itself. That's why this system needs rotation. Switch up what the tokens mean every few weeks. Sometimes they can be used for privileges, at other times stored for a team celebration, or even turned into "mentor credits," where older athletes coach younger ones. This variation keeps the brain from tying focus to one specific outcome and pushes it to rediscover the intrinsic value of attention.

After each week or cycle, include a short debriefing ritual where you spend three minutes journaling or reflecting on the experiment:

- *"When did my focus feel strongest?"*
- *"What distractions were hardest to resist?"*
- *"What did I learn about staying locked in?"*

You're shifting the reward from the token to the experience, not "bribing" yourself to pay attention, but pushing focus to become self-sustaining.

Wearables and Biofeedback

Lastly, it's time to see how we can safely bring tech into all this. Wearables surround today's athletes: watches that track heart rate, sensors that monitor movement, and apps that measure sleep quality. However, if used carelessly, these can become distractions or data overload.

For young athletes like yourself, the simplest and most effective biofeedback tools are heart rate (HR) and pulse checks. These connect physical sensations to mental states. After a drill or game, take 15 seconds to measure your pulse, either manually or through a basic wearable. Then, note how focused or calm you felt during that period. You'll notice patterns: maybe your best focus is when your heart rate is slightly elevated or when you breathe deeply before a play.

Manually Checking Your Pulse

This section is about tech, but what if you don't have a wearable that can detect your pulse? Here's a simple way to check:

- Place your right index and middle fingers on the inside of your left wrist, right under your thumb, *or* on the left side of your neck, under your windpipe.

- Press gently until you feel your pulse.

- Count the beats for 15 seconds. Note if they feel really fast.

- Multiply the number by 4 to calculate your heart rate (beats per minute).

Biofeedback Drills *(1 – 2 minutes)*

Pulse Check

1. Sit quietly, breathe slowly, and check your pulse.
2. Focus on lowering it through breath control and grounding.
3. Then, jump into a quick, intense task (like throwing, dribbling, or passing).
4. Recheck your pulse and reflect: did your focus hold steady?

Muscle Relaxation

1. Stand or lie down in a comfortable position.
2. Tense all your body for five seconds. Then release.
3. Next, focus on different muscle areas (shoulders, neck, legs, face, fists) and tense each group before relaxing it.

Deep Breathing

1. Sit or stand with your back straight.
2. Place one hand on your chest and the other on your belly.
3. Inhale slowly through your nostrils, letting your belly expand first, rising, then your chest.
4. Hold your breath for three seconds.
5. Exhale slowly through the mouth, letting your chest fall first, then your belly.

These teach **sensation awareness:** the ability to feel when your body is in a focused state versus when it's scattered. Once you can *sense* focus, you can create it faster.

However, there is one non-negotiable: ***privacy and consent***. All wearable or biofeedback tech use must be voluntary and transparent. You need to understand precisely what's being tracked, how it's stored, and who sees it. If you're under 18, coaches and parents must approve this data use. No one should ever feel pressured to share biometric data for training purposes.

Focus isn't about blocking everything out. It's about understanding what to let in. You train it through awareness, structured challenges, creative games, and constructive feedback. Each time you purposefully manage your attention, even for a few seconds, you're strengthening your control.

In the next chapter, you turn to the following mental toughness pillar: **Emotional Regulation**. You'll explore how arousal mapping works once you understand your optimal zone of performance, learn some breathing/anchoring tools, and the benefits of stress inoculation.

Key Takeaways

- Attention and focus vary depending on age, sport, and the role within the sport. The ideal way is to practice switching between narrow focus and broad attention, depending on what the situation requires.

- Auto-triggers, micro-cues, and reset protocols all work on "snapping back" your focus, whether before a game, in-play, or after mistakes and fumbles.

- Constraints-led approaches to attention involve gradually increasing constraints or conditions that force selective attention to practice focus in different scenarios, as a team or an individual.

Champion Mantra:

"The athlete who controls attention controls the outcome."

Chapter 3: Emotional Regulation and Arousal Control

In sports, emotions and energy can make or break your performance. Some days, you're going to feel flat and disconnected, while on others you'll be so fired up you can't think straight. Both extremes hurt your game. The goal is to find your sweet spot, your middle ground where your body is ready and your mind is clear.

This isn't a constant fight between "being calm" and "getting pumped." Your energy is more like a dimmer switch or a volume knob. You just need to learn how to tune it just right. Too low, and you can't bring your A-game. Too high, and you lose control. Sports psychologists call this **arousal regulation**. Athletes train it using tools from acceptance-based approaches (learning to notice your emotions without fighting them) and biofeedback research, especially **Heart Rate Variability (HRV)** training, which helps you sense and control your body's stress signals.

Arousal Mapping and Emotional Literacy

The Arousal Curve for Youth Athletes

The **inverted-U model** or **hypothesis** depicts your energy as an upside-down U. On the left side, you're too sleepy, distracted, or low-energy. On the right side, you're overly tense, anxious, or jittery. The peak's top is your **optimal zone**, where your mind and body work in sync.

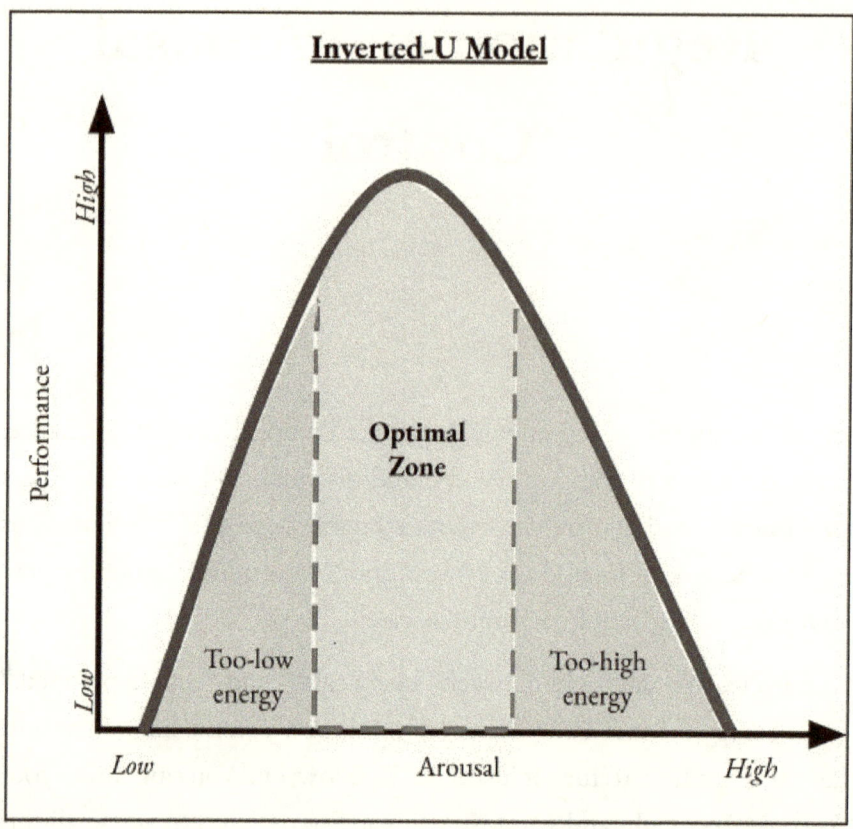

Think of yourself as Goldilocks eating the bears' porridge:

- *Too Cold (Low Arousal)*: You move slowly, respond late, and feel heavy.

- *Too Hot (High Arousal)*: You're boiling over, heart pounding, thoughts racing, maybe even snapping at teammates.

- *Just Right (Optimal Arousal)*: You're locked in, alert but calm.

The key is knowing what "just right" is for you. Every athlete has their own pattern, their own "U" that traces when their energy is too high and when it's not enough.

Field Test: Finding Your Functional Zone

1. Before a practice or game

Rate how "amped" you feel on a scale from 1 (barely awake) to 10 (heart pounding):

1	2	3	4	5	6	7	8	9	10

2. Afterward

Rate how you performed, from 1 (terrible) to 10 (phenomenal):

1	2	3	4	5	6	7	8	9	10

3. Compare your scores over a week or two.

You can even add the numbers to a graph to see where your "U" lands on the energy scale. You'll start to notice a pattern. Maybe you play your best around a 6 or 7 on the arousal or "amped up" scale. Perhaps you play best near 4 or 5. That's your **functional zone**.

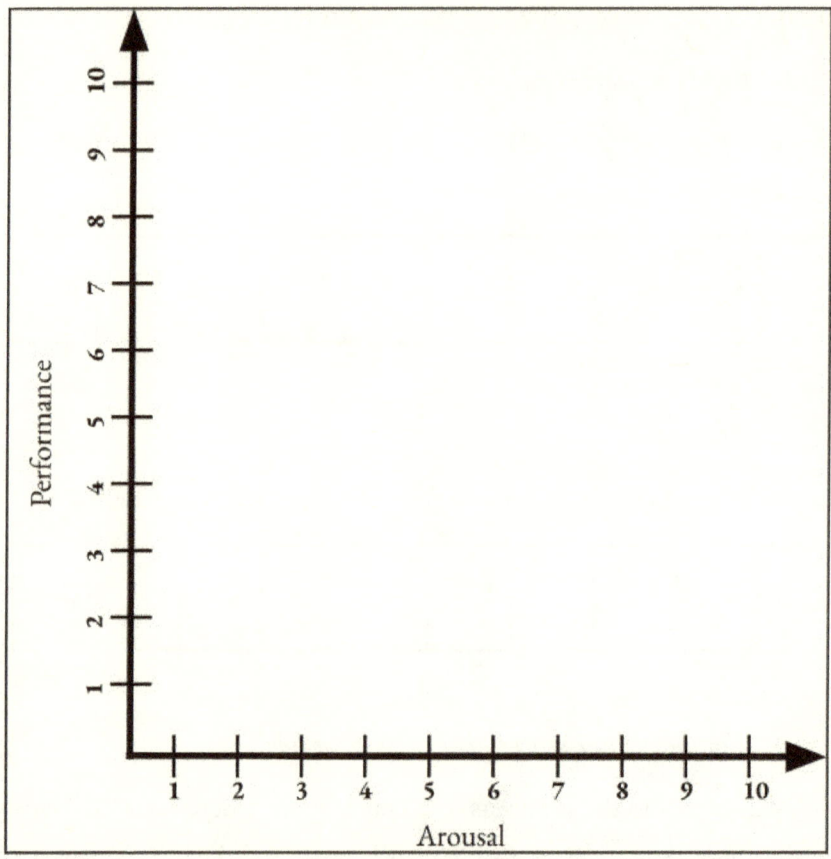

To make this more real, pay attention to your **body cues**. HRV-based biofeedback training teaches athletes to track subtle signs in their heart rate, breathing rhythm, muscle tension, and even how their hands feel.

For example:

- When you're too low, your breath might be shallow, your body heavy, and your thoughts distracted.
- When you're too high, your chest might tighten, your breathing quickens, and your movements are jerky.

- When you're in your zone, your breath is steady, your body feels light but firm, and your focus feels automatic.

Document your cues and write them down alongside your quantitative data:

- *"What did I feel before and during my best moments today?"*
- *"What signs told me I was too flat or too tense?"*

Over time, this builds your personal **arousal map**: a self-awareness tool you can use before any performance.

Build Your Emotional Vocabulary

Once you can detect your energy levels, the next step is to name your emotions, because you can't manage what you don't understand.

Athletes often use vague labels like "I'm off," "I'm fine," "I'm stressed." But **emotional literacy**, the ability to identify and describe your emotions, gives you precision.

To turn this confusion into clarity, we're going to start simple.

You'll create a 10-word feelings map with ten basic emotions and one physical cue for each. The purpose of the cue is that you can immediately tell what emotion you're currently feeling when you notice what's happening with your body.

Below is a sample:

Emotion	Physical Cue
Calm	Slow breathing

Focused	Steady gaze
Excited	Heart beating faster
Nervous	Tight stomach
Angry	Clenched jaw
Frustrated	Hot face
Confident	Upright posture
Bored	Slumped shoulders
Happy	Relaxed body
Annoyed	Constant sighing

For younger kids, you can make it a bit more fun by using emojis to visualize each feeling:

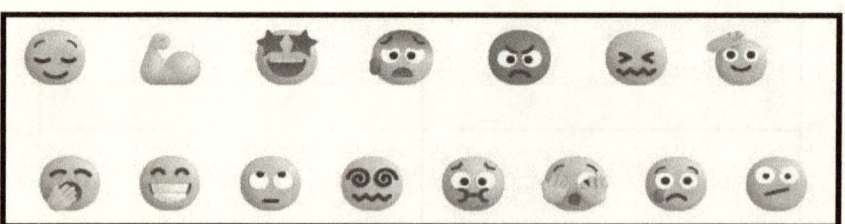

A color chart depicting different emotions and their branching feelings is another great way for young athletes like you to visualize each feeling and understand where you are in the emotional landscape:

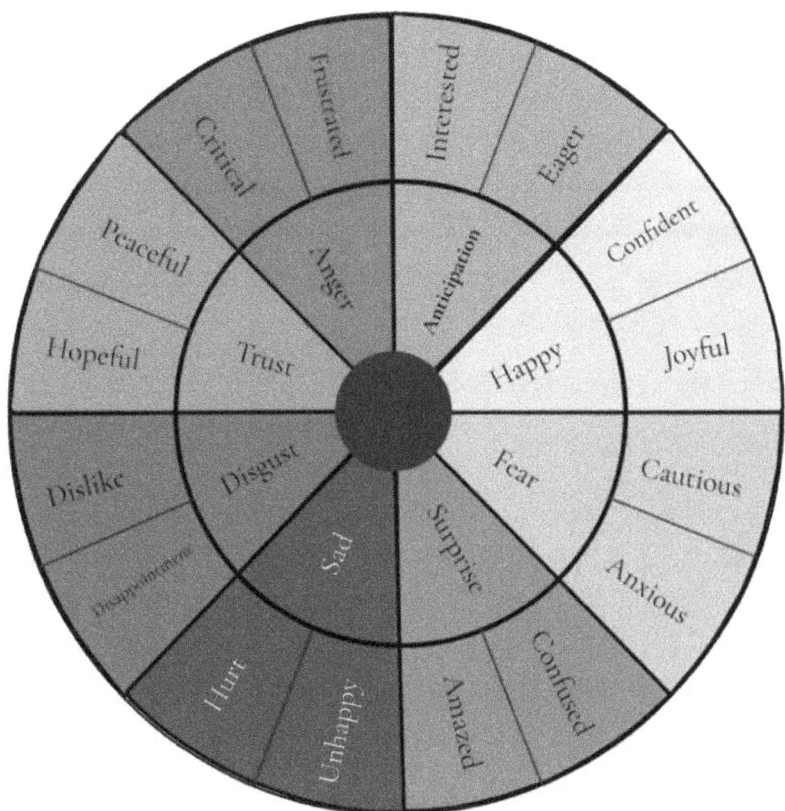

Younger athletes can even act out their emotions with quick role plays:

- "Show me what 'frustrated' looks like."
- "Show me 'calm.'"

This helps normalize emotions. Instead of thinking, "I shouldn't feel this way," you switch to, "What am I feeling? What does this tell me about my mind or body?" Your emotions are feedback from your body. They tell you what state you're in so you can adjust.

By naming and responding rather than reacting, you practice what acceptance-based therapy calls **mindful awareness**: seeing emotions as passing experiences, not problems to be solved.

Red Flags and Escalation Protocols

Being a young athlete can be very stressful at times. The pressure of competition, the build-up of other responsibilities, just having off days- it all piles on. Self-regulation is good, but sometimes we can't see what's happening when we're in the thick of it. This is why you need a healthy support system of coaches and parents who will keep an eye out for red flags that are telling you to *slow down*.

Here are a few signals coaches and parents can watch out for:

Behavioral Red Flags

- Sudden withdrawal, mood swings, or loss of interest in usual activities.
- Steep decline in motivation, focus, effort, or performance.
- Outbursts of anger, aggression, irritability, or crying.
- Extreme self-criticism or frequent talk of failure.
- Withdrawing from teammates or skipping practice.
- Signs of bullying (victim *or* aggressor)

Physical Red Flags

- Unexplained injuries or repeated "accidents."
- Noticeable fatigue, weight changes, or poor hygiene.
- Persistent illness, headaches, or stomach issues without a medical cause.
- Difficulty falling asleep or staying asleep

Psychological Red Flags

Expressions of hopelessness, worthlessness, or wanting to "disappear."

Excessive fear of failure, perfectionism, or avoidance of competition.

Isolation and refusal to communicate.

School Red Flags

- Trouble focusing in class
- Declining grades

Documentation Form for Coaches/Parents				
Date	Behavior Change	Possible Trigger	Action Taken	Follow-Up

Sometimes, all coaches/parents need to do is ask if you're okay, check in with you constantly, and encourage you to keep going. Listening calmly and validating your feelings while keeping you safe is the number-one priority. However, coaches/parents should not diagnose or offer solutions if they do not know what the inherent problem is, and they should *definitely* not ignore warning signs or mental health issues.

Always encourage openness regarding mental health and encourage athletes to pursue these channels if they're feeling stifled. School counselors and mental health coordinators are also integral parts of the team and system, and you should treat them as such.

Occasionally, there might be dire situations that require immediate escalation by coaches and parents. As a young athlete, you might not recognize the unsafe environment you're in, or you might suppress anything you feel is a threat to your performance. That's natural and expected, which is why your network is filled with support and open communication.

Emergency Escalation Situations

Mentions or signs of self-harm or suicidal thoughts.

Disclosure or suspicion of abuse or neglect.

Serious threats toward others or violent behavior.

Medical emergencies or suspicion/disclosure of substance abuse.

In scenarios like these, it's crucial to prioritize the athlete's safety and contact the necessary services for immediate intervention.

A good way to keep these protocols open and transparent is to provide athletes with a contact list of anyone they might want/need to reach out to, so that everyone knows who might be contacted in any emergency situation.

Contacts Info		
Role/Service	Name	Phone/Email
Safeguarding Coordinator/Team		
Mental Health Counselor/Team		
Emergency Services		
Crisis Helpline		

Safe Scripts for Supportive Conversations

Starting a conversation about emotions can feel awkward, but it's crucial. Remember to use non-judgmental open language that invites honesty.

Coach to Player:

"I noticed you were a little off lately. Anything stressing you out? No pressure, I just wanted to check in."

Parent to Athlete:

"You seemed tired the past few days. How's your sleep? Is something bothering you at school or at practice?"

Teammate to Teammate:

"You looked frustrated after that drill. Want to talk about it or just take a break?"

These scripts are just examples of the kind of language to use to communicate safety and empathy. No one's going to open up if they feel judged, belittled, or controlled. The goal is to normalize emotional talk the same way we talk about sore muscles or nutrition.

Fast Regulation Tools

When emotions rise, your body often reacts before your brain even catches up. That's how we're wired. It's time we start working *with* these reactions.

The following techniques are backed by HRV research. Basically, it involves how your heart rhythm reflects your stress level and recovery ability. High HRV means you're calm and steady, while low HRV typically means you're tense and reactive.

Breathing and Micro-Posture Resets

Your breath is the fastest remote control for your nervous system, sending instant messages to your brain about safety or threat. Shallow, quick breaths often indicate a 'fight or flight' instinct. Deep, slow breaths imply confidence and surety.

Remember: Just breathing during high-pressure moments doesn't work. You need to *train* your breathing before you need it, so it becomes automatic. If you only practice regulation when you're stressed, your system won't trust it. The key is repetition under calm conditions—before practice, in class, or while brushing your teeth. You're teaching your body that this pattern *means* calm and in control. Later on, your nervous system's "muscle memory" will kick in.

4-2-6 Breathing

- Inhale through your nose for 4 seconds.

- Hold for 2 seconds.
- Release your breath gently through your mouth for 6 seconds.
- Repeat three to five times.

That longer exhale activates your 'rest and digest' system, lowering your heart rate and improving HRV. The short pause in the middle helps you feel the control.

Box Breathing

- Inhale for 4 seconds.
- Hold for 4 seconds.
- Exhale for 4 seconds.
- Hold for 4 seconds.

This simple, rhythmic breathing is like drawing a square in your mind and helps you regain stability. It's great for when you need focus and control before a key play, a free throw, or a serve.

Pair Breathing with Posture Cues

When you combine your breathing with physical cues, your body position can also tell your brain how to feel.

- Exhale all the air out.
- Roll your shoulders back, feel your spine tall (confidence).
- Lift your chin (awareness).
- Unclench your jaw and your hands (for safety and relaxation).
- Inhale deeply for 4 seconds.

Together, your breath and body language form a micro-reset you can do anytime between plays or during a timeout.

Cognitive Reframes and Quick Scripts

Your body may react first, but it's your *mind* that decides what that reaction means. That's where **cognitive reframing** comes in: changing the story you tell yourself in the moment.

3-Word Reframes

- *"This is practice."*
- *"Breathe, then act."*
- *"Calm equals power."*
- *"Patience yields focus."*
- *"Now, next play."*

When pressure hits, short, punchy scripts like this are the best. These act as mini mental resets, fast enough to interrupt spirals before they take over.

Mini Stories

Sometimes, a single line isn't enough. That's when you use mini-stories that have personal meanings to help you stay grounded.

- *"Pressure is just proof that I care."*
- *"The nerves mean my body's getting ready."*
- *"This moment is my test run, not the final test."*

The idea is to flip the emotion from a threat to a challenge. Science shows that athletes who interpret stress as energy perform better and recover faster. It's not the *emotion* that hurts you; it's the *meaning* you attach to it.

Convert-the-Thought Exercises

1. Write down a common unhelpful thought: *"I always mess up under pressure."*
2. Convert it → *"Pressure is my cue to breathe."*
3. Say it out loud.
4. Repeat with your teammates, your coaches, or turn it into a group challenge.
5. By doing this often, your brain learns to automatically swap fear scripts for fear scripts.

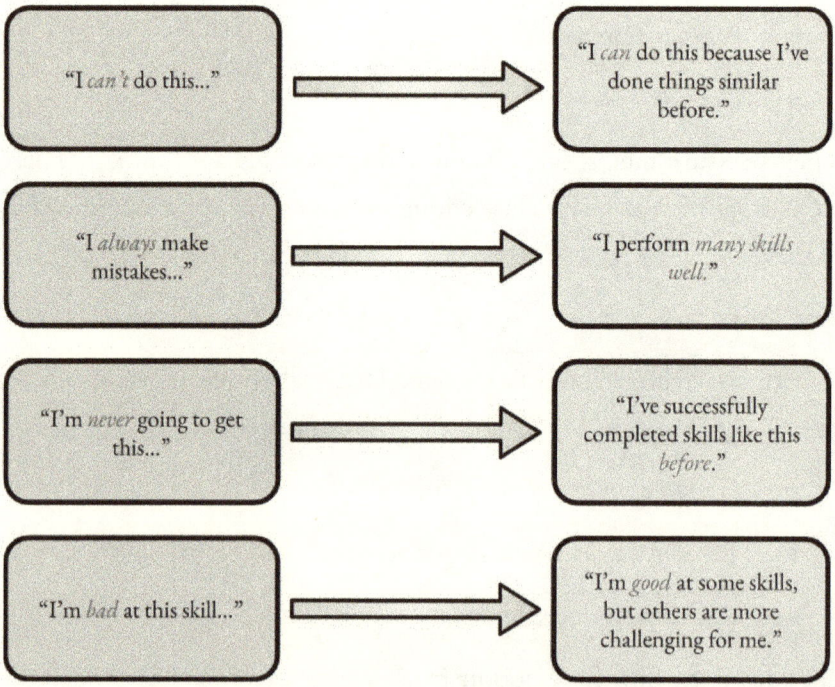

If you're playing a team sport, reinforcing this process with team language can really help bring everyone together and forge a bonded team. Teams that share reframes perform more consistently, the shared language acting as a collective regulation cue.

Anchoring and Exposure Micro-Training

Stress hijacks us sometimes at the most unexpected and annoying times. Staying grounded under that pressure by training your system is the ideal way to handle it.

Neutral Anchors

An **anchor** is a physical cue (like a touch, gesture, or word) you pair with a calm, focused state until the two become instinctive together.

For example:

- Lightly pressing your thumb and forefinger together.
- Touching your wristband.
- Tapping your chest once (or the body part that currently feels tense).
- Whispering your cue words.

Building an anchor:

1. Sit in a calm state (after a breathing exercise or during some downtime).
2. Do your chosen anchor while breathing slowly for 30 seconds.
3. Repeat this daily for a week.
4. Also, use it purposefully *right after* your breathing resets at any time during the week.

Soon, your brain links that cue to that same calm state. Then, in a real game, you can trigger the sensation with just a touch or a word.

Pressure Lab: Short Exposure Sessions

To really make these tools work, you have to stress test them to be certain they'll hold up under real pressure.

You simulate the pressure in small, controlled bursts so your body learns how to stay balanced.

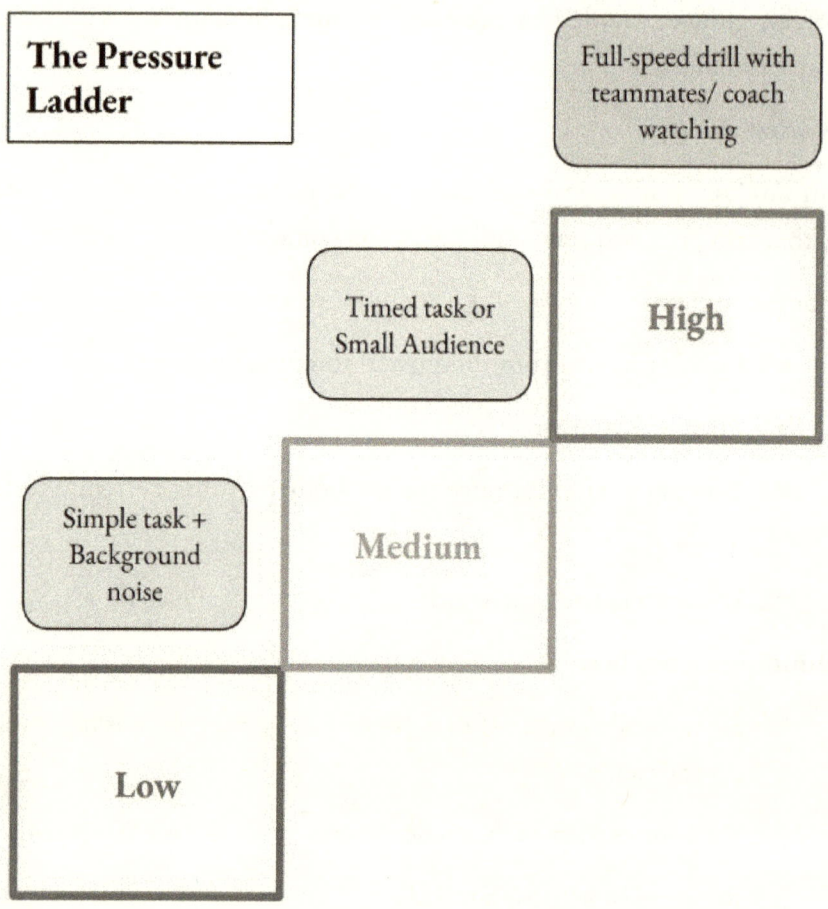

In each step, use your tools (breathing, posture, reframes, anchors, etc.). Notice how your system reacts to the increasing levels, then resets.

It's also important to reflect after these micro-sessions (or, as a coach, to debrief your players):

- *"What did I feel first?"*
- *"What helped me reset?"*
- *"What cue worked fastest?"*

This locks in the learning, helping you see the patterns and what works best for you. Maybe your breath is your best reset, or your anchor word hits faster.

The point is *awareness*. The better you understand your system, the faster you can guide it.

Quick Recap

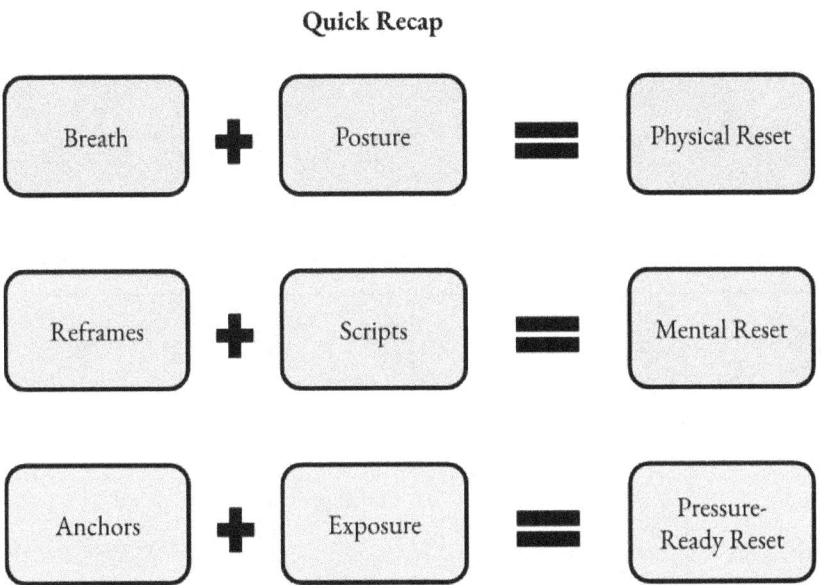

Building Enduring Emotional Resilience

We've recognized our emotions and learned how to regulate them in different moments. It's time to take all of this and use it to create long-lasting and self-sustaining emotional and endurance systems within us.

Stress Inoculation Cycles

Think about how vaccines work: your body learns to fight off real viruses by facing tiny controlled doses. **Stress inoculation** works the same way for your mind and emotions. Rather than avoiding the stress, you train *with it*, little by little, so that when the real stress hits (championship game, missed play, big crowd), your system already knows how to handle it.

The cycles work by gradually increasing exposure to controlled challenges. You learn to recognize stress signals, like a racing heartbeat or tense muscles, breathe through them, and return to your optimal zone. HRV training shows that athletes who regularly practice regulation under mild stress build higher **physiological flexibility**, meaning they can bounce back from emotional and arousal spikes.

Designing Stress Cycles

Remember to increase challenge levels gradually as your confidence grows and integrate them into your season's schedule.

Week 1–2: **Controlled Micro-Stress**	Add time limits, short pressure drills, or mini competitions. *E.g.:* 30-second shooting challenge with teammates watching. After, take one 4-2-6 breath.
Week 3–4: **Moderate Stress Simulations**	Integrate realistic scenarios, like crowd noise, mock interviews, or simulated 'losing score' moments. Pair these with posture resets and cue words.
Week 5–6: **Full Pressure + Debrief**	Run full-game simulations under fatigue. Record your responses: - What triggered stress?

	- What helped you reset?

After each cycle, hold a short debrief circle with your team or coach (or just yourself) for two to three minutes. Discuss and reflect on what worked, what didn't, and what regulation tools helped. One by one, you'll notice tolerance gains as you have fewer emotional 'highs' and faster recovery.

Tracking Progress

Below is a sample tracker to help you see your endurance build over weeks with consistent reflection and self-evaluation. You could use a wearable to measure your heart rate, or you could manually calculate it.

Week	Stress Dose/ Simulation	Intensity (1–10)	Regulation Strategy Used + Recovery Time (mins)	Pre-Stress HR	Post-Stress HR
1	*E.g.: Timed drill + noise distraction*	4	*4-2-6 breathing* *6 mins*	*67 bpm*	*134 bpm*

Reflection / Notes	*Felt nervous, but recovered quickly*

2						

Reflection / Notes	

3						

Reflection / Notes	

4						

Reflection / Notes	

5						

Reflection / Notes					
6					
Reflection / Notes					

Sleep and Recovery's Role in Regulation

You can't regulate your emotions or build endurance if your body is running on empty. If you have to put your phone on charge, then you need to do the same with your body.

In other words: *sleep*.

When you sleep, your brain processes memories, your hormones rebalance, and your HRV stabilizes, all directly affecting how calm *or* reactive you'll be the next day. According to researcher Matthew Walker in his book, *Why We Sleep*, even a single night of poor sleep can lower emotional control and increase negative mood reactivity.

So, how much should you sleep?

- *Ages 13–15:* 8.5 to 10 hours of sleep per night.
- *Ages 16–18*: 8 to 9 hours of sleep per night.

> ***Tip!***
>
> Regular sleep beats long sleep. A consistent bedtime (within a 30-minute window) improves emotional stability more than sleeping longer at random times.

Wind-Down Rituals

(15–30 minutes)

Your brain needs a signal that it's time to shut down. Try blocking out 15 to 30 minutes before bed for calming cues and to unwind.

- *Tech-off Zone*: No screens 30 minutes before bed (blue light suppresses melatonin)
- *Body Reset*: Gentle stretching or a few minutes of slow breathing.
- *Mind Dump*: Write three thoughts in a journal: things you're grateful for, worried about, or want to remember.

Checklist for Sleep Debt

Sleep debt is the difference between the amount of sleep you need *and* the amount you actually get. Sometimes, it can be hard to figure out if you're sleeping well, so here's a checklist:

- ☐ Woke up without an alarm (more than twice a week)
- ☐ Needed caffeine or energy drinks to "push through" the day.
- ☐ Zoned out during school.
- ☐ Was irritable, snappy, and/or foggy during practice.
- ☐ Had increased soreness, fatigue, or reaction time lag.
- ☐ Fell asleep at different times during the week.
- ☐ Woke up at different times during the week.

If you checked two or more, you're likely running a sleep deficit. Recovery starts by resetting your schedule, even by 15 minutes earlier each night.

Recovery Interventions

It's time to pay off our sleep debt before it gets too big to handle and becomes a chronic sleep deficit.

- *Power Naps*: 20 to 30 minutes (never longer) before 4 p.m.
- *Post-Game Nutrition*: Protein and carbs within 45 minutes of play.
- *Cold-to-Warm Contrast Showers*: 30 seconds cold, then 60 seconds warm for three rounds to lower cortisol and balance HRV.

Travel Tips

Sports occasionally take you on the road with your family and/or your team. Sleep can sometimes be lost in the mix of bags, check-ins, and training.

- *Pack Routine Cues:* Use the same pillowcase and small blanket, or include a scented candle to signal 'sleep mode.' (Use this consistently *before* travel, so it's actually effective on the road.)

- ***Keep Pre-Sleep Rituals Consistent***: Even in hotels, stick to your wind-down routine, whether it's journaling, stretching, or listening to calming music.

- ***Hydrate Early, Not Late***: Avoid chugging water right before bed on travel days to avoid waking up in the middle of the night.

Rituals for Emotional Closure

Emotions don't disappear when ignored- they build up in the body, waiting to burst. **Emotional closure** is the act of intentionally wrapping up a practice, game, or season so your nervous system and mind can reset.

Post-Practice Micro-Circles

1. Circle up (either with your team, fellow athletes, or coaches), and everyone shares one word about how they feel.
2. Take one deep breath together.
3. Repeat as many times as needed for *everyone* to feel calm and collected at the end.

Three-Minute Processing Prompts

These can be done solo or as a team. After challenging games or a particularly grueling practice, use a question to start reflecting and processing the emotions that came up.

For example:

- *"What emotion hit hardest today? What did it teach me?"*
- *"What went right, even if the score didn't?"*
- *"How can I reset before tomorrow?"*

This trains emotional literacy (understanding what you feel and why), which is a key predictor of resilience.

Journaling for Emotional Processing

Journaling helps shift emotions from the mind to paper, freeing up mental space.

A standard format for journaling is to start with a one-line recap of the day, then rate your feelings on an effortless emotion scale. This pushes you to be mindful and contemplative, narrowing your focus on the simplistic things you feel or do. Then you can use a prompt (see suggestions below). Your writing doesn't have to be deep or long. Even 60 seconds can build awareness loops that signal to your brain that emotional recovery is possible.

Simple Emotion Scale

Journaling Prompts

- What's one thing you appreciated about today's challenge?
- What went well today, even if it was small?
- What effort are you proud of, whether it worked out or not?
- What moment stood out the most today? Why?
- When did you feel more like yourself?
- When did you feel off-balance or disconnected?
- Is there something you wish you'd done differently? What can you learn from it?
- What do you want to let go of before tomorrow?

- How can you be kinder to yourself about something that didn't go perfectly?

Some athletes carry heavier emotional loads. In these cases, coaches, team captains, and parents can hold private check-ins with them. These are quick, supportive chats that open space for honesty.

It's essential to maintain a non-judgmental atmosphere. There's no shame in needing extra help or mental health support, and coaches should model that behavior. Making sure athletes are safe, mentally and physically, is the top priority. One-to-one communication is integral to ensuring everyone has the support they need.

Even one safe conversation can prevent emotional overload and show that resilience isn't a solo skill, but a team effort.

The secret isn't being emotionless. Through emotional regulation, you learn how to use your feelings intelligently, steering them to the most beneficial path. Biofeedback is a reminder that you can *see* your nervous system's rhythm change through breathing and awareness.

Now, it's time to turn to the third pillar of mental toughness, understanding how confidence and identity perception affect performance. Here, you'll be introduced to mastery logs, self-talk scripts, and narrative identity exercises, all of which are designed to enhance your self-efficacy.

Key Takeaways

- Emotional literacy is an essential skill for athletes, as it helps them understand their optimal energy and performance zones and learn to use emotions as data rather than hindrances.
- Breathing tools, cognitive reframes, and anchoring are great methods to train in low-stakes situations, gradually increasing the pressure to adapt to higher optimal zones.

- Stress inoculation cycles are effective ways for athletes to build emotional resilience, gaining tolerance for pressure while learning to unwind.

Champion Mantra:

"Too calm or too hyped, both lose. Find your sweet spot."

Chapter 4: Confidence, Identity, and Self-Talk

With daily doses of small successes and problems solved, you build a portfolio of confidence. Often, people think that mental toughness simply means having a lot of confidence. However, that's not the case. The confidence that comes with mental toughness involves showing up when things are difficult and drawing strength and belief in yourself from the reserves you've built up each time you need to perform.

Psychologist Albert Bandura (1997) called this belief in your ability to influence outcomes **self-efficacy**. It's the confidence that "I can figure this out." The key to gaining this self-efficacy isn't empty compliments or vague hype, but is based on *evidence*.

Here, you'll learn how to build up that evidence within yourself to draw on it at any point.

Building Evidence and Mastery

Mastery Logging and Evidence Banks

This will be your personal 'proof of progress' system. Instead of waiting for someone else to tell you you're improving, you'll show yourself the evidence. According to Bandura (1997),

"Athletes need efficacy-affirmation evidence that they can exercise better control over their performance attainments with cognitive aids than without them." (p.376)

The Daily 3-Line Mastery Log

Each day, take two minutes at the end of practice to record three short lines:

Day 1	**What I did** (Something specific you worked on or overcame)	*E.g.: I stayed calm after missing my first serve.*
	Why it mattered (The value or lesson behind it)	*I didn't spiral so that I could reset and recover points.*
	Next step (What you'll do tomorrow to build on it)	*Practice breathing reset between serves tomorrow.*
Day 2	**What I did**	
	Why it mattered	
	Next step	
Day	**What I did**	

3		
	Why it mattered	
	Next step	
Day 4	What I did	
	Why it mattered	
	Next step	
Day 5	What I did	
	Why it mattered	
	Next step	

Day 6	What I did	
	Why it mattered	
	Next step	
Day 7	What I did	
	Why it mattered	
	Next step	

This simple reflection builds **narrative identity**: the story you tell yourself about who you are becoming. Over time, those three-line entries become evidence that you're capable and disciplined.

Evidence Bytes

In addition to writing about your progress, research has shown that *seeing* yourself in action (with appropriate evaluative and instructional feedback to *understand* what you're seeing) is a potent tool for skill acquisition and building self-efficacy. The important thing here isn't to highlight what you might've done *wrong*, but to focus on how good the performance is and how to do it *right*.

Once you've visualized and conceptualized how a skill is performed, seeing your body execute it can help you develop your proficiency.

Record short 10 to 20-second video clips that capture your progress, whether it's landing a new skill, finishing a challenging workout, or speaking up in a team huddle. Save them all in an 'Evidence Bank' folder. Watching your own growth and literally seeing the proof makes your progress feel *real*. It strengthens the belief circuit in your brain. On days when doubt hits, rewatch a few clips to remind yourself: "I've done difficult things before."

The Weekly Review

Once a week, scroll through your log and clips and highlight your top three wins.

Reflect:

- "*What patterns am I noticing?*"
- "*What habits helped me succeed?*"
- "*What challenges keep repeating?*"

This review will turn the scattered moments you've gathered into a story of progress, which, in narrative identity theory, is precisely how confidence solidifies. You start viewing yourself as someone who is *becoming* confident, not just someone who is *trying* to be.

Attribution Retraining

When something goes right or wrong, your brain instantly searches for a reason, or an **attribution**. The explanations you choose shape your confidence, often more than the event itself.

Bandura found that confident people (or, as he put it, people with "perceived self-efficacy") don't avoid failure; they just explain it differently. They attribute success to **controllable attributions** ("I practiced, I focused") and view setbacks as **changeable** ("I didn't plan well enough this time"). People who lose confidence often do the opposite; they blame fixed or external factors (**uncontrollable attributions**) ("I'm just bad at this," "The coach hates me").

The first step to retraining this is to *learn the difference.*

Event	Uncontrollable Attribution	Controllable Attribution
You miss a penalty.	"I always choke under pressure."	"My focus slipped. I'll be sure to add breathing drills this week."
You ace a serve.	"I got lucky."	"I practiced consistently this time."
You lose a game.	"The ref was unfair."	"We didn't adjust our defense early enough."

Confidence grows when you concentrate on what you can control, which is your effort, preparation, focus, and recovery.

Reattribution Practice

After either a win or a loss, it's vital to reflect on it, attributing *both* to things within your control. That way, with wins, you can mark your progress and outstanding performance, and note down areas you can continue to improve. With losses, you take accountability and remember that losing isn't a sign of failure, but something that can be worked on.

Reflection Prompts:

1. "What happened?"
2. "What did I do that helped or hindered?"
3. "What can I repeat or change next time?"

Example:

1. *I missed my target in the last round.*
2. *That was because I rushed my setup.*
3. *I could add a pre-shot breath cue next time to slow down.*

Do these enough times, and your inner dialogue starts shifting from criticism to curiosity.

Team Controllables Drill

If you're in a team sport, it can be beneficial to remind each other of controllable attributions. This helps stop the 'blame game' after mistakes or losses, helps identify areas for development, and creates a collective sense of victory with wins.

With your team, list what's inside vs. outside your control before a game:

Inside	Outside
Mindset	Refs
Effort	Weather
Focus	Opponents Attitude
Communication	Crowd Atmosphere

Then, as a group, agree to discuss only **controllables** during games. This normalizes a growth-oriented team culture and builds collective confidence, as Bandura called it, **collective efficacy**.

Micro-Competence Ladders

Big wins aren't all that bring confidence. Stacking small wins consistently grows your self-efficacy. Imagine a video game with levels that get harder each time you beat one. Each small success keeps you engaged, with just enough of a challenge to stay motivated but not so much that you feel crushed.

That's how your training should feel.

Break Big Goals into Micro-Tasks

Big goals can be intimidating and vague. That's why you should take any skill and divide it into small, winnable steps:

- Instead of "get faster," aim for "improving the first 5m sprint start."

- Instead of "get mentally tougher," aim for "holding your focus for three reps before reset."

It's a bit of a cliche, but remember to keep your micro-goals SMART, which will help in tracking your progress:

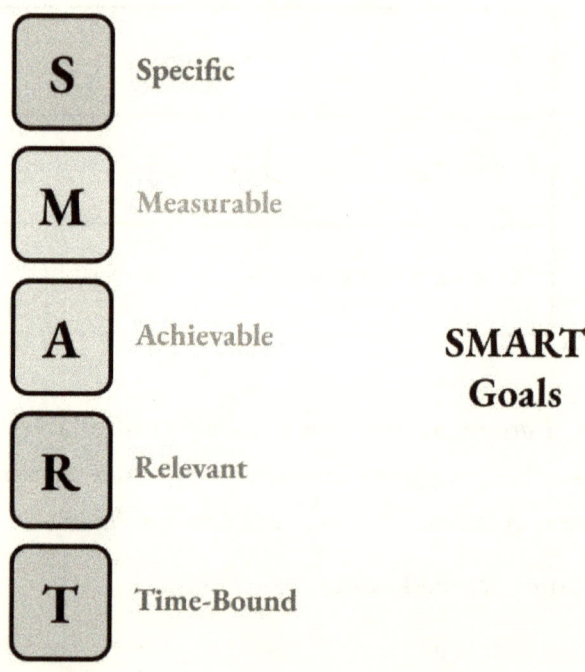

Rotate Tasks to Stay Sharp

After a few repetitions of micro-tasks and goals, the brain adapts and can become **complacent**, that is, used to the level of difficulty and no longer learning/growing. That is why it's essential to *rotate* every week or two and introduce fresh challenges. These keep your nervous system engaged and prevent stagnation in your confidence.

For example:

- *Week 1:* Accuracy focus.
- *Week 2:* Speed under pressure.

- **Week 3**: Combine both in a mini-simulation

Build Feedback Loops

Each micro-task needs a fast feedback system:

- If you're training solo, use a stopwatch, a mirror, or a quick self-rating (1–10).
- If you're on a team, use partner check-ins or short peer notes.

When feedback is immediate, your brain connects cause and effect faster ("I adjusted my breathing and improved accuracy"). That instant connection strengthens self-efficacy circuits.

Plus, positive feedback loops reinforce positive, controllable attributions. On the other hand, not receiving any feedback (resulting in thoughts spiraling) or receiving negative feedback will lead to focusing on uncontrollable attributions and self-doubt.

Feedback Loop

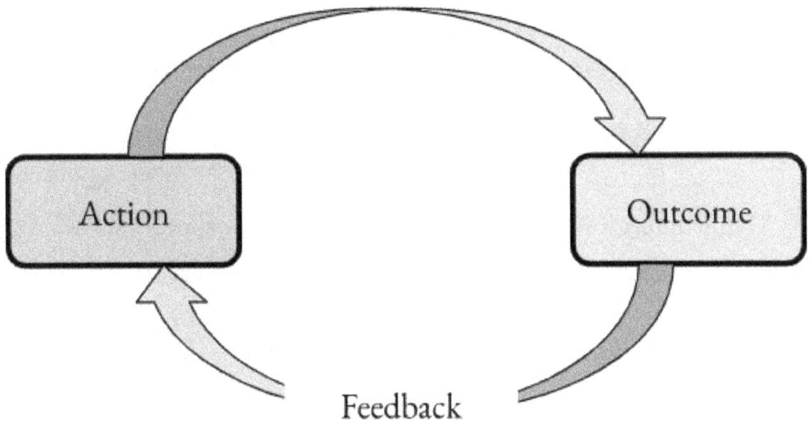

Self-Talk and Sensory Anchors

Pre-Play Scripts

Think of your mind as your personal locker room. What you say in it before stepping onto the field, court, or stage sets your mindset for the game. A **pre-play script** is like your game plan for confidence. It's short, personal, and action-based, built to remind your brain who you are and what you do best.

Formula

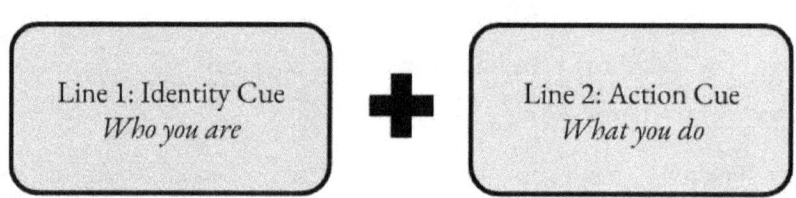

Examples:

- *Soccer Player:* I'm a calm playmaker. + I see the field and make the pass.
- *Gymnast:* I trust my body. + Every move has flow.
- *Basketball Guard:* I lead the court. + I set the pace.

Notice how each script uses the **present tense** and **active verbs**. It's not "I *will* set the pace," but "I *set* the pace," "I *see*," or "Every move *has*." That's intentional. Bandura's work on self-efficacy shows that confidence grows from mastery experiences and self-verbal persuasion—the words you choose literally teach your brain what to expect from you.

"It requires undaunted belief in one's efficacy to sustain the effort needed to convert potentiality into athletic proficiency." (Bandura, 1997, p.384)

Once you've written your script, you *must* train it. Say it out loud before practice, before drills, and before scrimmages. The goal isn't just to "sound" motivational or to repeat empty words. It's to make your language automatic. Every repetition builds an evidence deposit that strengthens your self-efficacy bank. Then, *test it under pressure.* When you use your script during scrimmages or mock performances, you begin to notice how it feels: is it too long? Too soft? Too generic? Keep adjusting it until it clicks.

Remember: Confidence scripts aren't one-size-fits-all; they evolve with your growth. You'll know it's right when it feels like second nature.

Refinement Process

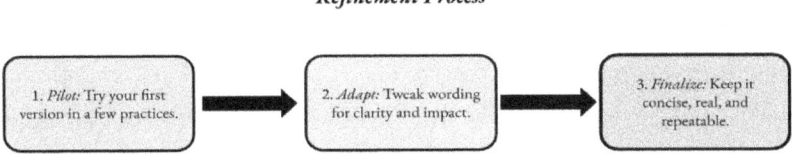

Handling Negative Loops

Everyone talks to themselves, but not everyone realizes just how loud and influential that voice can be. Self-talk can become a **loop**: a thought repeats, reinforces itself, and shapes your performance. A single "I always mess this up" can replay and, over time, build a belief. The solution isn't forcing blind positivity right away, but gradually moving negative loops from neutral to empowering.

Managing Negative Loops

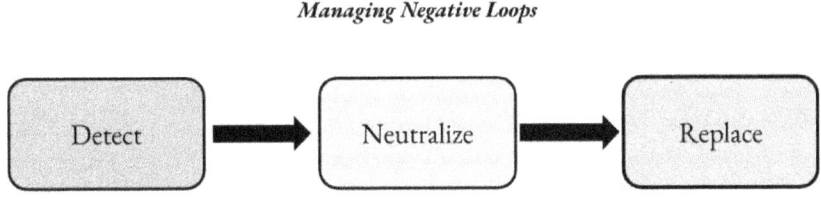

Step 1: Detect the Loop

Start noticing your internal monologue, especially after mistakes. Are your thoughts harsh? Do they use words like 'always,' 'never,' or 'can't'? That's your first signal that they may be negative. Awareness alone starts reducing the loop's hold.

Step 2: Neutralize It

You can't jump straight to "I'm amazing!" from there. Your brain won't believe it. Go *neutral* first. Turn "I always choke under pressure" to "I'm learning to handle pressure." Neutral self-talk removes judgment and keeps the focus on growth.

Step 3: Replace with Empowering Language

Once neutral feels natural, upgrade to empowering. "I'm learning to handle pressure" becomes "I thrive under pressure." The phrasing feels earned because it was built on small wins. This shift mirrors Bandura's **mastery principle**: absolute confidence grows through experiences that prove capability.

Example Sequence

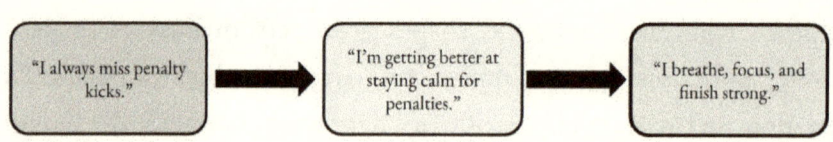

To make this process faster, *pair the replacement with a* **physical anchor**: something you can do instantly when pressure spikes. It could be tapping your chest, snapping a wristband, or letting out one deep exhale with a reset word like "steady." This combination of mental and physical action turns a mental habit into a conditioned reflex. The body cue tells your nervous system that you're safe and it's time to reset. One by one, the mind will follow the body's lead.

For team environments, try **peer-pair practice**. Partner with a teammate to rehearse switching loops. One player says a common negative thought ("I keep losing focus."), and the other helps reframe it to neutral or empowering. It's surprisingly fun, motivating, *and* it builds collective awareness. The more your team normalizes mental resets, the more substantial group confidence becomes.

Sensory Confidence Anchors

Now let's add another layer: your **senses**. The brain learns through words *and* association, particularly smells, sounds, textures, and even colors. A **sensory confidence anchor** is a physical or sensory cue that links to a calm and confident state.

Examples:

- *Sound*: A short song clip or rhythm you hum before a play.
- *Touch*: A wristband, smooth stone, or patch you rub or press.
- *Scent:* A subtle essential oil or scent patch you use only during training.

When you repeatedly pair a specific sensory cue with a steady or focused state, your brain will link the two. Later, when you're under pressure, triggering that same cue recalls the feeling fast. It's a simple application of **classical conditioning**: the same principle that trains your brain to associate your alarm tone with waking up.

Step 1: Condition It in Calm

Never start establishing this sensory anchor when you're chaotic. Choose your cue and pair it with a confident moment- possibly during breathing practice, visualization, or light stretching before practice. Make sure your body is relaxed and your thoughts clear and steady as you establish the cue. Hold the cue (touch, sound, or scent) for a few seconds as you focus on your calm state.

Step 2: Test It Under Mild Pressure

As soon as your brain links the cue to calm, test it in low-stakes situations: a timed drill, a scrimmage, a quiz, or even a challenging workout. Use your anchor any time your heart rate rises. Notice how quickly it helps you reset.

Step 3: Apply It in Real Performance

When it's game time or performance day, use your anchor right before your pre-play script. It helps center your nervous system before the mind takes over.

Step 4: Rotate Anchors to Avoid Overuse

Like any tool, anchors can wear out if used too often or without intention. Your mind and body get used to them, and they no longer serve their intended purpose. Rotate between different sensory types (sound, touch, scent) to keep their effect fresh. The goal isn't to rely on them forever, but to train your system to self-regulate faster.

Anchors are especially powerful for teens because your nervous system is still developing its regulation speed. You're basically training your brain's circuit to respond on demand, a skill that transfers beyond sports to tests, performances, or social stress.

Narrative Identity and Rituals

Athlete Story work

Every athlete has two stories: the one you tell others and the one you tell yourself. The second one, the internal story, is what truly shapes your identity. Narrative identity research adds to Bandura's idea of self-efficacy by stating that we build this belief through the stories we tell about our lives, how we explain our challenges, our effort, and our growth.

Your story doesn't have to be long. In fact, start with one powerful paragraph, answering the question, *"Who am I becoming?"* This is not a perfect version of who you are.

> *"I'm becoming the kind of player who keeps composure under pressure, who brings energy even when the score's against us, who shows his teammates that consistency beats talent."*

That's it. One small paragraph that connects identity to behavior. The point is to give your brain a narrative anchor. When you can name who you're becoming, your habits make more sense. You're no longer just doing drills or showing up early; you're reinforcing your story.

Who am I becoming?
_____
_____
_____
_____
_____
_____

When you write it, the next step is to *practice* it like a skill. Say it out loud before games or workouts. Keep it in your locker or notes app. Then you start *updating it* quarterly. Every few months, review your story and add objective evidence. What did you do that proved you were growing into that person? Maybe you led a warm-up, handled a mistake better, or encouraged a teammate when you were tired. Write those details down.

This process builds **mastery evidence**: small wins that strengthen belief in your capabilities.

Role Rituals to Embody Identity

Now that you've written who you're becoming, it's time to *embody* it. This is where **role rituals** come in: short intentional actions that help you step into your identity. Think of them as physical or symbolic switches between roles, like an actor getting into character when they yell "Action!"

Pre- and Post-Rituals

- A quick locker gesture: touching your number before walking out.
- A short mantra you whisper before the whistle: "Calm, ready, attack."
- A deep breath and posture reset before you sub in.
- A wrist tap that suggests 'game mode on.'

These tiny rituals create psychological cues that tell your mind and body that it's time. They strengthen what psychologists call **embodied cognition**: the use of your body to influence your mindset. The more you use them, the more these cues become habits, helping you access your confident identity on demand.

Rituals can also mark *transitions* in your journey.

For instance:

- After an injury, your return-to-play ritual might be putting your brace on with intention and saying, "I'm ready to rebuild."

- If you're benched, your ritual might be a deep breath and a commitment phrase: "I learn while I wait."
- After a challenging game, your ritual could be journaling one learning point before leaving the locker room.

Here, the ritual serves as a cue to shift from a passive identity (on the bench or injured) to an active one (learning to play or recovering).

Moreover, when teams use rituals together, they create a **shared identity**. These could be group chants, huddles, or even a moment of focused silence before stepping on the field. This isn't based on superstition, but a synchronizing belief and purpose. Even pro teams do this, from handshakes to slogans to game-day routines. They're not random; they're tools to trigger a collective mindset.

Celebrations that Reinforce Process

Most people celebrate outcomes—wins, trophies, medals—but resilient athletes also celebrate *the process*. This is one of the most significant differences between temporary confidence and durable confidence. Bandura would say process celebrations build **efficacy loops**: moments that reward effort, learning, and persistence, which feed motivation for the next challenge.

These should be meaningful, no matter how small. For example, you could place a 'learning wall' in your locker room: a space where teammates write one lesson learned from each game, scrimmage, or training week. Or weekly 'shout-outs' during practice for someone who stayed after to improve a skill. These micro-ceremonies don't take long, but they change how people define success.

Families can do this too. Instead of "Did you win?" ask, "What did you work on today?" or "What moment made you proud?" Over dinner, celebrate *effort over outcome*, as these are the small habits that align with growth. This kind of recognition builds **internal validation,** so confidence comes from your own behavior rather than external praise.

To make rituals and celebrations sustainable, you can use low-cost or symbolic tokens:

- A colored wristband for each skill milestone.
- A small token is added to a team jar after every shared process win.
- A note of appreciation left in a teammate's locker.

These tokens make the invisible visible. By marking progress, they act as proof that the process *itself* is worthy of celebration.

When done enough times, these rituals form a feedback system that connects identity, action, and reward. You *act* like your best self, *notice* it through rituals, and *reinforce* it through the narrative/story. This loop fuels long-term confidence and cohesion, in sport and in life.

Narrative Loop

Identity → Action → Reward

Reinforce

Confidence isn't just about hyping yourself up. It's about building the proof that you can rely on yourself, reinforcing that with anchors and cues, and solidifying it as part of your identity through the story you tell. That's the power of narrative identity: your story becomes your strategy.

We're going to keep this mental toughness a little longer. In the next chapter, you'll dive further into shaping your identity and motivations through constructing your goals. You'll understand the different SDT principles for goal architecture, how to set up micro-goals, and establish systems based on your season.

Key Takeaways

- You learned that the basis of self-efficacy and confidence is evidence and focusing on controllable attributions. By using mastery logs, video clips, scripted prompts, and feedback loops, you tracked your progress.

- You combined language (self-talk scripts) with sensation (anchors) to teach your brain confidence through multiple pathways. This gradual process will, in time, turn negative thoughts into empowered ones.

- You established your identity through looking to the future, rejecting perfectionism, and focusing on realistic shifts and growth. Because of this, you now celebrate the process instead of the outcome.

Champion Mantra:

"Confidence is a portfolio: build it with daily deposits."

Chapter 5: Motivation and Goal Architecture

One of the factors under the mental toughness pillar of Confidence is **motivation**. You see, motivation is what gets you started, that spark when you set a goal or picture a future version of yourself. We touched on goals and future projections in the last chapter, focusing on narrative identity. However, motivation is a much more complex concept, as it can fade. Fast.

The real key to long-term progress is what you build *around* that motivation: the systems, habits, and mindset that keep the engine running even when you don't feel like showing up. Here, you're going to learn how to *stay* motivated by designing a structure that makes motivation sustainable.

Researchers Edward Deci and Richard Ryan call this kind of motivation "self-determined." Their **Self-Determination Theory (SDT)** shows that humans stay motivated when three needs are met: **autonomy** (the feeling of choice and control), **competence** (the sense of growth and ability), and **relatedness** (the feeling of connection). Add Carol Dweck's research on the **growth mindset** (the belief that abilities can be developed through effort and learning), and you've got the foundation for what we'll call your **goal architecture**.

Motivational Fundamentals

Support Autonomy, Competence, and Relatedness

1. *Autonomy*

Let's make something clear: Autonomy doesn't mean doing whatever you want. It doesn't mean you can be selfish or arrogant.

It means feeling like your choices matter.

When coaches or teachers let you make small decisions, like picking your warm-up song, choosing between two drills, or deciding your role in a team project, your brain feels more ownership. You're not being forced to participate; you're *choosing* to. That sense of ownership flips motivation from **extrinsic (external – *"I have to do this"*)** to **intrinsic (internal – *"I want to do this"*)**.

"Comparisons between people whose motivation is authentic (literally, self-authored or endorsed) and those who are merely externally controlled for an action typically reveal that the former, relative to the latter, have more interest, excitement, and confidence, which in turn is manifest both as enhanced performance, persistence, and creativity…This is so even when the people have the same level of perceived competence or self-efficacy for the activity." (Deci & Ryan, 2000, p.69)

Apply This:

In your next practice, ask yourself, "What's one small decision I can take ownership of today?" Maybe it's how you structure your warm-up or what skill you focus on first. Autonomy grows from micro-decisions like these.

2. *Competence*

Competence is the need to feel capable and improve. It is built through micro-tasks: small, achievable goals that stretch your skills slightly beyond your comfort zone (remember the SMART goals). If you try to jump from level 1 to level 10 instantly, you'll get frustrated, demotivated, and lose drive. However, when you master one small challenge at a time, you get constant feedback that reinforces the feeling that "I'm getting better."

"The theory argues, first, that social-contextual events (e.g., feedback, communications, rewards) that conduce toward feelings of competence during action can enhance intrinsic motivation for that action. Accordingly, optimal challenges, effectance-promoting feedback, and freedom from demeaning evaluations were all found to facilitate intrinsic motivation." (Deci & Ryan, 2000, p.70)

Apply This:

Instead of "I need to run a 5K without stopping," break it down into smaller, more competent tasks: run for five minutes, then eight, then twelve. Each time you hit a new mark, you build evidence of progress.

3. *Relatedness*

Relatedness is the feeling of being connected to others. You might not realize it, but team chemistry, inside jokes, positive coaching, and shared rituals all boost motivation. Humans are wired to belong. When you feel supported by teammates, coaches, or family who believe in you, you push harder and recover faster from setbacks.

"The primary reason people initially perform such actions is because the behaviors are prompted, modeled, or valued by significant others to whom they feel (or want to feel) attached or related. This suggests that relatedness, the need to feel belongingness and connectedness with others, is centrally important for internalization." (Deci & Ryan, 2000, p.73)

Apply This:

In a team setting, design a simple 'challenge chain.' Each week, a different teammate sets a challenge for the group (like five perfect passes in a row or a no-complaint day). You'll notice that motivation spreads faster when a shared goal connects everyone.

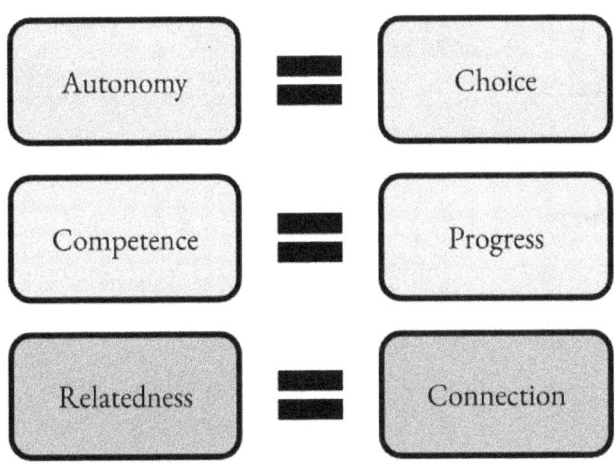

SDT's Fundamentals for Intrinsic Motivation

When all three align, motivation becomes self-sustaining. You're no longer chasing rewards, but growing for your own reasons.

Growth Mindset Interventions

Now that your motivational structure is built, it's time to keep it flexible. That's why you need to maintain a **growth mindset.**

Psychologist Carol Dweck found that people with a growth mindset believe their abilities can improve through effort, feedback, and persistence. In contrast, those with a fixed mindset believe talent is either innate or not. The difference sounds small, but it changes everything about how you react to mistakes.

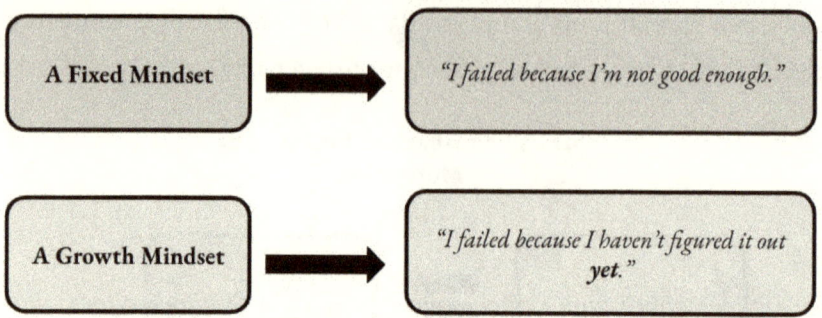

The one word (yet) is very powerful

Failure Framing Exercise

Next time something doesn't go your way (a bad game, a low score, a missed opportunity), write out this sentence:

> I didn't achieve [GOAL] _____ yet because I'm still learning how to [SKILL] _____.
> My next step is to _____
> _____
> _____
> _____
> _____
> _____

Process Praise Scripts

This is another simple growth-mindset tool. Rather than focusing on results ("You're so talented!"), Focus on effort and strategy ("You really stayed composed during that drill," or "You found a better way to solve that problem.") You can use this on yourself, too. After tough sessions, try saying,

- *"I stayed patient."*
- *"I improved my decision-making."*
- *"I found a workaround."*

These short scripts help train your inner voice to value effort over outcome.

Coach Calibration

Coaches, parents, or even peers play a role here as well. Knowing *when to challenge* and *when to comfort* is key. If someone is discouraged and needs confidence, comfort helps them re-engage. If they're playing it too safe, challenges push them forward.

The best mentors balance both: firm on standards, flexible in support.

You can practice this balance with teammates. When someone's down, don't just say, "It's fine." Combine comfort and challenge: "You had a rough day, but I know your passing is better than that. Let's figure out how to fix it next time."

Values Mapping and Alignment

Motivation fades when goals feel empty or disconnected from what you care about. That's why it helps to **map your values**: the deeper reasons that make your daily effort meaningful.

Values are your internal compass. They guide choices even when no one's watching. Once you know your top values (the ones you prioritize), you can design habits that express those values in action.

Value Cards

Choose three from the following values that feel the most like *you*. Write one way you can live each value during practice or school.

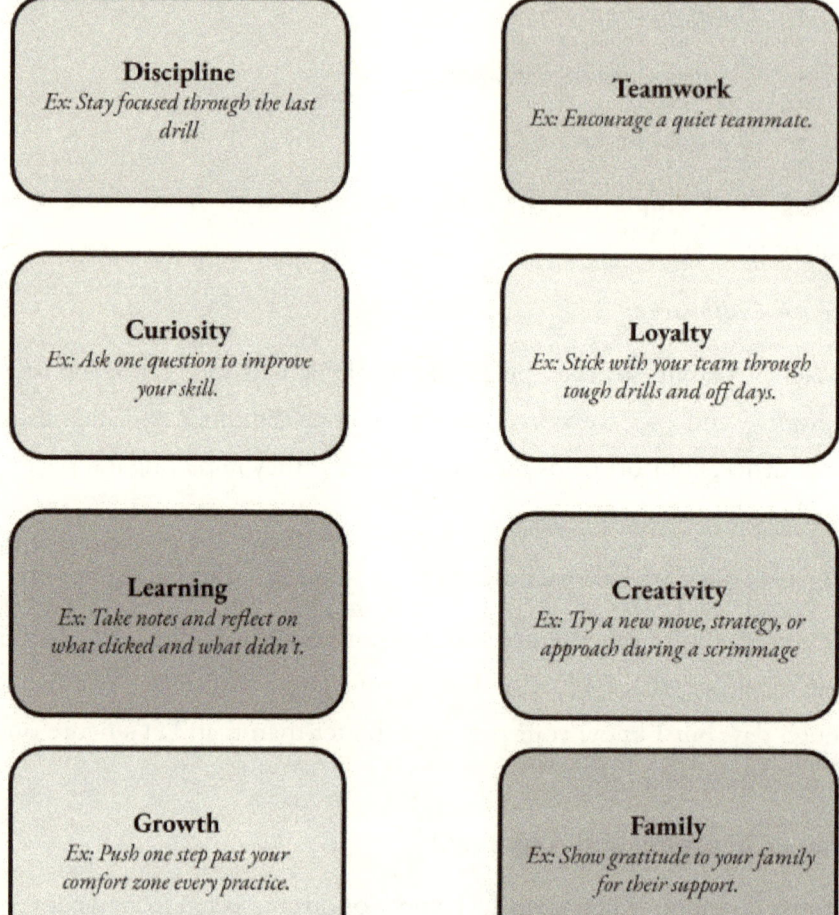

Values also make great **anchors** during tough sessions. When you're tired, unmotivated, or frustrated, remind yourself: ***"Why does this matter to me?"***

That question often reignites purpose faster than external rewards.

For example, if one of your values is 'Family,' think about how your effort represents them and the pride they feel watching you grow. If your value is 'Growth,' remind yourself that challenges are proof you're stretching beyond limits.

Parent/Coach Scripts

Adults around you can also strengthen your motivation by linking praise to values rather than just to results. "Good job scoring" can become:

> *"I loved how you kept helping your teammates. That shows real leadership."*

You can do this for yourself, too, when reviewing your day or journaling. Note where your actions matched your values. That self-recognition builds intrinsic motivation, the kind that doesn't depend on trophies or approval.

Goal Architecture and Micro-Goals

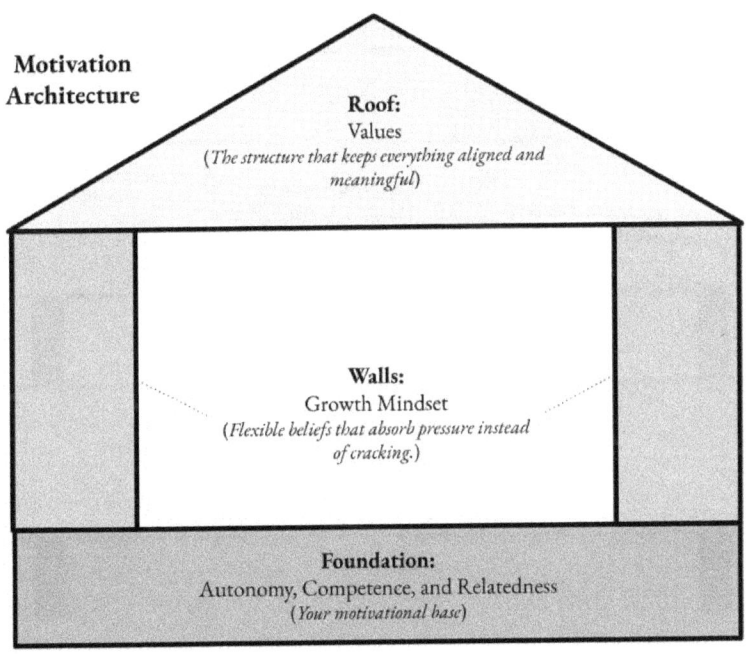

Just as your motivation is built, so are your goals. The **outcome** is the top floor, what you see from the outside. The **performance goals** are the beams and floors that support it. The **process goals** are the bricks you lay down every single day. You can't jump straight to the top floor without building the structure beneath it.

Many young athletes fall into **outcome fixation**: they only care about the win, the score, or the highlight. The problem is that outcomes are often outside your control. You can play your best game and still lose, or practice really well and get a tricky judge. When your self-worth is only tied to results, your motivation wobbles.

To break that cycle, you need a *three-tier scaffold*:

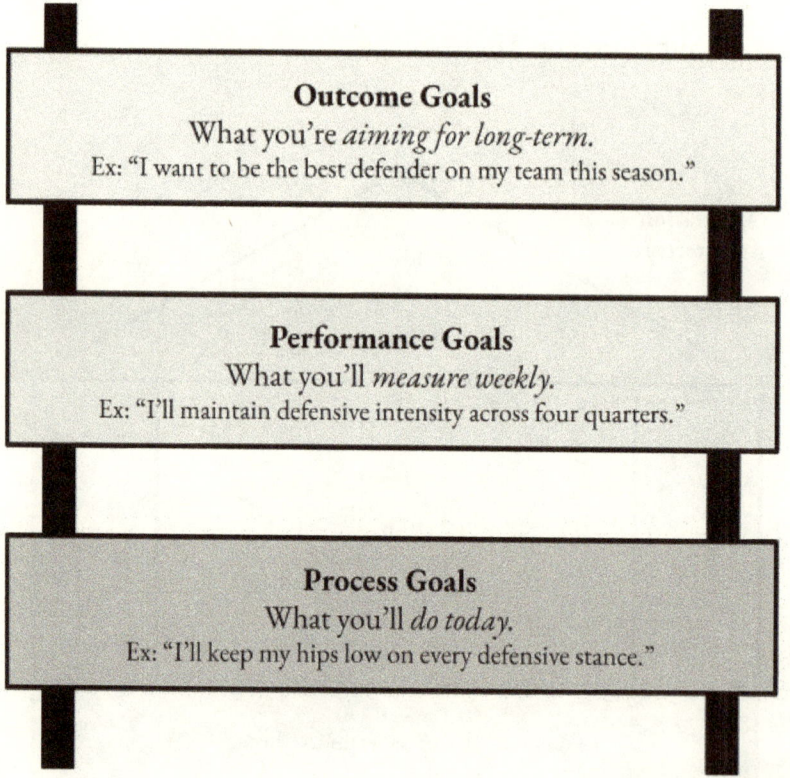

The 3-Week cycle

Instead of setting vague goals like 'get better,' organize your progress in 3-week cycles:

- **Week 1**: Observation and Setup. Track your habits, learn your weak spots.
- **Week 2**: Apply and test your process goals. Make minor tweaks daily.
- **Week 3:** Evaluate performance goals. Check what improved and what stalled.

Then, reset the cycle. Keep what worked and adjust what didn't. This rhythm prevents burnout and keeps your motivation fresh.

Every week, set one checkpoint (a mini-review moment):

- *"What process habit did I follow most consistently?"*
- *"What skill metric actually changed?"*
- *"What's one tweak I'll make next week?"*

If something didn't work, don't scrap the whole system. Just adjust one rule. For example:

"If I skip a workout, I'll do a shorter 10-minute mobility session instead."

- **Long-term cycle outcome goal:**_____

    Ex: Improve consistency in free throws by the end of the season.

- **Performance focus for 3 weeks:**_____

    Ex: Raise my free-throw average from 60% to 70%.

- **Key process focus (controllables):**_____

Ex: *25 perfect-form free throws after every practice.*

Week 1: Observation and Setup (Build Awareness)	
Day / **Process Goal (Daily Habit)**	**Reflection/Notes**
Mon	
Tue	
Wed	
Thu	
Fri	
Sat	
Sun	***Weekly Checkpoint:*** What did I notice about my habits or focus?

Week 2: Application and Adjustment (Do + Refine)		
Day	Performance Check (Measured Skill)	Reflection/Notes
Mon		
Tue		
Wed		
Thu		
Fri		
Sat		
Sun		***Weekly Checkpoint:*** What improvement did I see? What needs refining?

Week 3: Measure, Evaluate, and Reset			
Day	Process Goal (Daily Habit)	Performance Check (Measured Skill)	Reflection/Notes
Mon			
Tue			
Wed			
Thu			
Fri			
Sat			
Sun			***Weekly Checkpoint***: Did I reach my target? What's my next 3-week goal?

Micro-Goals, Streaks, and Momentum Systems

Big goals can feel exciting until they start feeling *too big*. That's why micro-goals are more effective in keeping your engine running.

Each day, write down three micro-goals you can *realistically* complete. These should be things you can *control*; not whether you score 20 points or win a scrimmage, but whether you practice your footwork, reset your focus, or spend 10 minutes visualizing success.

For example:

1. *"Review yesterday's drills for 10 minutes."*
2. *"Hit 90% of my warm-up routine with full focus."*
3. *"Reflect on one moment I improved during practice."*

These are small enough to win daily, but meaningful enough to build **momentum**. Plus, your brain loves progress. That's why tracking your daily streaks works so well. Every time you complete a micro-goal, mark an X, color it in, or log it in an app. Seeing your consistency triggers dopamine (a reward chemical that reinforces your behavior).

After you hit a streak (say 7 days or 21 days), give yourself a short celebration or a moment of recognition. It doesn't have to be huge. It could just be saying, "Nice job. I'm building real discipline," or sharing your streak with a teammate. This all ties back to SDT, where autonomy and competence feed inner drive and intrinsic motivation.

When Streaks Break

The truth is that every streak *will* break eventually. You'll get sick, travel, forget, or just have a bad day. The important thing is to remember that that's not failure. It's more data you can use to grow.

Instead of punishing yourself, ask:

- *"What pattern led to the break?"*

- *"What cue or system can I change to make success easier next time?"*

For instance, if you keep missing morning runs, maybe your cue needs to move, like setting your shoes by the bed instead of in the closet. Each broken streak teaches you something about your habits and environment.

Day	Daily Goals	Weekly Streak
Mon	1. _____ ○ 2. _____ ○ 3. _____ ○	
Tue	1. _____ ○ 2. _____ ○ 3. _____ ○	
Wed	1. _____ ○ 2. _____ ○ 3. _____ ○	
Thu	1. _____ ○ 2. _____ ○ 3. _____ ○	
Fri	1. _____ ○ 2. _____ ○ 3. _____ ○	
Sat	1. _____ ○ 2. _____ ○ 3. _____ ○	
Sun	1. _____ ○ 2. _____ ○ 3. _____ ○	

Linking Goals to Cues and Routines

Notebooks are all well and good, but goals live in *actions*. To make your goals stick, link them directly with cues and routines in your daily life.

If-Then Planning

"If-then" plans turn goals into automatic responses. You won't simply rely on remembering to stretch or visualize, but you'll set up triggers.

For example:

- **_IF_** I put on my cleats, **_THEN_** I'll take three deep breaths to lock in focus.
- **_IF_** I finish practice, **_THEN_** I'll jot down one thing I improved.
- **_IF_** I get nervous before a competition, **_THEN_** I'll repeat my two-line self-talk script.

One-Sentence Mission Cards

To keep your goals fresh in your mind, write a one-sentence mission statement that sums up who you're becoming. Keep it on a card or on your phone background. Read it before practice or competition. That quick reminder reconnects you to your purpose.

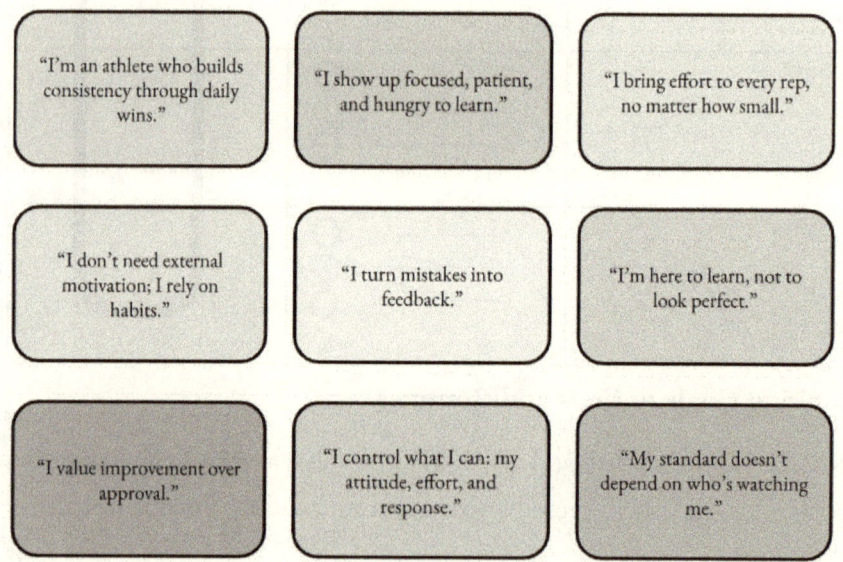

Accountability Pairing

Even the most disciplined people need accountability. Find a partner (a teammate, sibling, or friend) to check in with once or twice a week. Shake your three micro-goals and streak chart.

Ask each other:

- *"Did you follow your process goals this week?"*
- *"What's one small win you're proud of?"*
- *"What's one area you're adjusting next cycle?"*

Accountability works best when it's positive and consistent. You're not *guilting* each other, but supporting each other's progress and amplifying **relatedness**.

Season and Career Planning

Periodizing Mental Load

You already know that athletes plan their physical training in cycles, building intensity, tapering, then recovering. But your mind needs the same kind of structure. Just like your muscles, your brain can't stay at max intensity all season long. **Mental periodization** means aligning your mindset, focus, and motivation cycles with your physical ones.

Your season is split up into phases: some weeks are about pushing limits, others are for skill refinement, and some are for recovery. During high-intensity physical phases (such as preseason conditioning), mental training should emphasize sharpening focus and managing fatigue. During lower-load weeks, you can switch gears by reviewing your progress, practicing visualization, or setting up short-term goals.

Deloading Weeks for Mental Recovery

These are planned breaks for your mind, not just your body. During these weeks, you step back from the constant stress and pressure of competition. You can journal, spend time doing non-sport hobbies, or hang out with friends and teammates without an agenda. It's like letting your mind catch its breath. According to SDT, mental recovery protects your sense of autonomy and competence.

Pressure Inoculation Timing

This is when you intentionally practice performing under stress. The goal here is to handle stress in controlled doses, but you need to practice this at the right time. Early in the season, pressure simulations (like clutch scenarios or mock competitions) help you build confidence before it really counts. Pre-taper (right before the championship phase), however, your mental load should shift toward composure and focus under fatigue. During the season, keep stress doses small, consistent, but not overwhelming.

You want to adapt, not collapse.

Preventing Plateaus and Boredom

Plateaus are those frustrating stretches when you're training hard, but progress feels stuck. Sometimes, the issue isn't physical; it's **mental stagnation**. Our brains thrive on novelty and challenge. When practice feels too repetitive, our motivation dips because our sense of growth fades.

1. *Novelty Injections*

Mix in unexpected drills, new teammates, or fresh environments.

If you're a soccer player, try futsal for a week to sharpen reaction speed.

If you're a swimmer, add relay races or goal-based sets.

Novelty keeps your brain guessing and your motivation system (especially competence and curiosity) activated.

2. *Role Swaps*

Switch roles during practice for a day.

If you're a striker, try defending.

If you're a basketball point guard, take a turn running drills as a coach.

Role swaps build empathy, expand tactical awareness, and reignite a sense of challenge. Plus, they strengthen relatedness by helping you connect with your teammates' experiences.

3.   **Short Competitions**

Mini-tournaments, intra-squad challenges, or timed skill games can bring back the fun intensity during mid-season slumps.

Make them creative:

- Backward free throws.
- Blindfolded passes.
- Obstacle dribbles.

Performance matters, but so does keeping playfulness alive.

4.   **Mid-Season Micro-Evaluations**

Every four to six weeks, take a quick self-assessment:

- *"What's working?"*
- *"What feels stale?"*
- *"What's one thing I could tweak this cycle?"*

This reflection helps you reframe goals before boredom turns into burnout. Don't wait for a coach to fix things. Take control of your learning process. Your coach will likely be supportive if you come to them and say, "Hey, I want to try something new this week because I feel like I'm not moving forward."

5.   **Coach Interventions**

Sometimes, coaches do need to step in and break the monotony. Good coaches introduce fun constraints, such as limiting touches, changing the game size, or assigning creative challenges ("you can only score after three passes"). These playful restrictions force adaptability, developing skills and problem-solving at the same time.

Growth Beyond Sport: Transferable Goals

The best part of being an athlete is that the habits you build in sports are training you for life far beyond the field.

When you learn to plan a season, you're really learning project management.

Handling stress before a match? That's emotional regulation.

Taking feedback is building resilience.

These are **transferable skills**: abilities that make you better not only as an athlete, but as a student, leader, or future professional.

Translating Sports Goals to Life Goals

Let's say your current goal is to improve your shooting accuracy by 10%. Translate that idea for school: how could you improve your essay scores by 10%?

The method is the same: set specific metrics, track progress, and review results. Sport teaches you systemic thinking, how small habits add up over time. You take that growth mindset with you into every part of your life.

Life Skills Modules

Your team or school might already teach this informally, but you can take ownership by building your own 'life-skill training modules.'

- *Time Management*: Plan your week around practice, recovery, and study.

- ***Interview Prep***: Treat job or college interviews like a competition. Practice your responses, control your nerves, and visualize success.

- ***Team Communication***: Learn to give feedback constructively, like a captain leading a huddle.

These modules connect to SDT, enhancing competence (you feel capable), autonomy (you're taking initiative), and relatedness (you learn how to collaborate).

Pathways Beyond Competition

Not every athlete plays forever, but you can still stay connected to sports. You could coach younger players, mentor a rookie, or volunteer at youth camps. These experiences help you build a continuous identity, a sense that your lessons and skills still matter even if your role changes.

Multi-sport exploration also prevents burnout and builds adaptability. A basketball player who tries track learns to pace themselves. A swimmer who surfs develops balance and creativity. Every new experience feeds your personal growth.

In the long run, success in sport isn't just medals and stats. It's transferable confidence, knowing you can learn, adapt, and thrive in any environment. As Deci and Ryan describe, true motivation comes from feeling that your efforts are meaningful, chosen by you, and connected to a larger purpose. And Dweck reminds us that your mindset is the bridge between sport and life. The same persistence that drives you through practice can drive you through exams, jobs, or even building your own business someday.

As we continue exploring this pillar of mental toughness, we move on to embodying these ideals through physical foundations, habit stacking, sleep hygiene, and ethical tech use.

Key Takeaways

- According to Self-Determination Theory, intrinsic motivation relies on autonomy, competence, and relatedness, all of which are connected to your values. When everything aligns, motivation fuels growth.

- Building goals is about creating a structure that supports you and makes it easier to sustain motivation. Process and performance goals are just as important, and often more critical, than outcomes.

- A growth mindset means believing that your abilities can expand through effort, strategy, and feedback.

- Athletes think in cycles, not finish lines. You periodize your effort, fight through plateaus, and build bridges between sport and everything else you do.

Champion Mantra:

"Motivation lights the fuse; architecture keeps the engine running."

Chapter 6: Habits, Sleep, and Physical Foundations

All the pillars we previously talked about and all the work we did on growth, whether in terms of focus, emotion regulation, confidence, or motivation, all fall flat if you're physically exhausted. You can't race against time, and you can't outperform fatigue. There are no tricks or hacks to squeeze more out of your body than it can do.

The only way around it is ***rest***.

Habit Architecture and Behavioral Design

Getting better is the goal of most athletes. However, what separates consistency from inconsistency is the architecture of habits, the invisible systems behind their daily actions. Motivation might light the fire, but habits keep it burning long after emotions fade.

Habit Stacking for Youth Athletes

Habit stacking means connecting new behavior to something you already do every day, so it's harder to forget and easier to repeat.

For example:

- After warm-ups, take 90 seconds for a breathing or focus drill.
- After brushing your teeth at night, do a quick reflection: "What did I learn today?"

- Right before practice, visualize your first great play of the session.

These actions take only 60 to 180 seconds, but they compound massively. Each time you repeat them, your brain builds stronger neural links, so that eventually they become automatic.

Visual cues and checklists can help keep you on track. Maybe it's a sticky note in your locker that says, "Breathe first," or a phone reminder labeled "Focus minute." These cues reduce decision fatigue because you don't have to think about *when* to do it. The trick is to build systems that make success easy and cumulative.

Daily Momentum Checklist	
Habit	**Done?**
Focus drill (60–180 sec)	☐
Hydrated through the day	☐
Tech off 30 min before bed	☐
Reflection: "One lesson from today."	☐
Encouraged a teammate	☐

Environmental Nudges

The spaces and surroundings you spend time in influence your habits and actions far more than most people notice. This is where **environmental design** comes in: shaping your physical spaces to work *for you* instead of *against you*.

Reducing **decision fatigue** (the little hesitations that delay good habits) is key. The less time you spend deciding, the more time you spend *doing*.

At Practice:

- Set up the area so players naturally move from warm-up to visualization to drills.

- Create a 'Focus Corner': a calm space where you can reset between sets or after mistakes.

- Have a minimal gear list prepared and keep any equipment within easy reach to make it easier to use.

- Use locker cues: small symbols or words (like "Reset" or "Present") taped inside your locker door as a mental trigger.

At Home:

- Have a tech curfew—screens off at least 30 to 60 minutes before bed.

- Create a 'Study Zone' separate from your bed. Your brain should associate your bed with sleep, not stress.

- Keep healthy snacks visible, like fruit bowls instead of chip bags. When the right options are easy to grab, you're more likely to make good choices automatically.

Even your bedtime routine can become an environmental nudge. Dim lights, slow breathing, maybe a two-minute stretch- all this tells your body, "Hey, we're shutting down now."

Simple Accountability

Staying consistent alone is tough. So, start with **buddy systems**. Pair up with a teammate to check in on small habits, like recovery logs, mastery logs, nutrition goals, and focus drills. Text each other quick reminders or share short wins like, "Hit my sleep goal three nights in a row!" This kind of accountability boosts motivation by adding a social element, as humans naturally thrive on connection. When someone else is watching, your consistency increases; psychologists call this the

observer effect: we tend to perform better when we know we're being noticed.

Publicly celebrating streaks (like "20 days of focus drills! Woohoo!") can be powerful, but make sure they're done safely and respectfully. If you're celebrating yourself, be sure it doesn't come off as arrogant or bragging, but simple joy and pride. If you're celebrating someone else's streak, remember that not everyone wants excessive attention. You can always focus on team-based celebrations: "This week, our team hit 85% of our sleep targets!"

Coaches can also play their part. A quick weekly sign-off or 5-minute review session can help athletes reflect and reset.

Remember: you're not *punishing* missed habits. You're clearing up your goals and encouraging growth.

Finally, rotate accountability partners every few weeks. That keeps things lively and prevents burnout. It also helps distribute the 'social load,' meaning no one person feels responsible for everyone else's success (an unfortunate burden often placed on the team captain). This way, you build more team trust and learn from different people's routines.

Sustainable Growth

Habit Stacking gives you the structure. → **Environmental Nudges** create the supportive space. → **Accountability Systems** provide the *social energy* to sustain it.

Practical Blueprint (Sample)		
Morning	**Habit Stack 1:**	*Ex: Visualize a thriving practice while brushing your teeth.*
	Nudge:	*Keep the journal and water bottle visible by the sink.*
Practice	**Habit Stack 2:**	*After warm-ups, take 2 minutes to breathe and focus.*
	Nudge:	*'Focus Corner' in the gym with calm colors or motivation cards.*
	Accountability:	*End-of-week review with your buddy or coach.*
Evening	**Habit Stack 3:**	*Write one sentence in your reflection log.*
	Nudge:	*Tech off 30 mins before bed. Stretch lightly.*
	Reward:	*Celebrate streaks in team chat.*

Sleep, Nutrition, and Movement

At the end of the day, all habits and skills rely on the same critical foundations: sleep, nutrition, and movement. If you don't fuel your body correctly, you can't expect it to keep running on a low charge.

Sleep Hygiene

People need sleep. That's not really a shocking revelation. However, Matthew Walker's *Why We Sleep* proves that sleep is not just rest, but active recovery. Your brain is locking in skills, repairing tissues, and balancing hormones that regulate energy and mood. You can't build consistency without restoration.

For athletes specifically, sleep affects:

- Reaction time (even one all-nighter can slow it by 20 to 30%).
- Injury risk (sleep-deprived athletes are up to 60% more likely to get hurt).
- Focus and decision-making (fatigue shrinks activity in your prefrontal cortex).

Now, if you're a teen athlete, your body is in one of the most crucial growth phases of your entire life. Generally, you need about **8 to 10 hours of quality sleep per night**. Skimping on sleep is going to make you tired *and* will literally block your body from performing at its full potential.

Recommended Sleep Windows

- *Under 13*: 9 to 11 hours per night.
- *Ages 13 to 18*: 8 to 10 hours per night.
- *College athletes*: 7 to 9 hours per night.

Consistent Wake-up Time: Even on weekends, try not to sleep in more than an hour past your usual wake-up time. Your body thrives on rhythm, and a steady schedule can improve your sleep quality without adding more hours.

Night Routine

Create a consistent wind-down routine:

1. ***Device Curfew***: Power down phones and gaming consoles at least 30 to 60 minutes before bed. The blue light tricks your brain into thinking it's still daytime, delaying the release of melatonin (your natural sleep hormone).

2. ***Wind-Down Breathing***: Try 3 to 5 minutes of slow breathing (in for 4 seconds, out for 6) or gentle stretching. This signals your nervous system to switch from 'fight or flight' to 'rest and digest.'

3. ***Low-Light Mode***: Keep lights dim after 9 p.m. Soft lighting tells your brain it's time to rest.

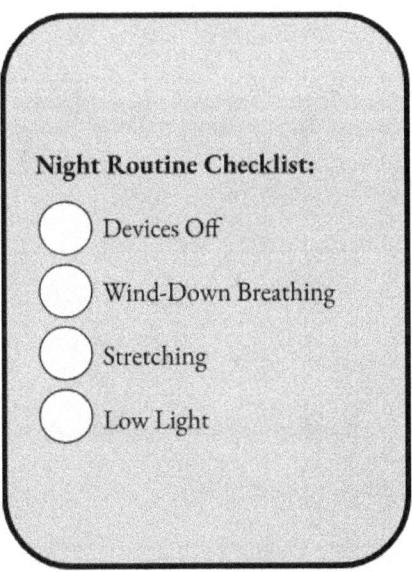

Travel Sleep Hacks

Athletes often travel early, sleep in hotels, have away games in different time zones, and play under bright lights, all of which mess with your circadian rhythm. To keep your recovery on track:

- ***Pack Sleep Tools***: an eye mask, earplugs, and your own pillowcase (for familiarity and hygiene).
- ***Anchor Your Routine***: Even if your bedtime shifts, keep your pre-sleep routine the same (Phone off, breathing done, low light).
- ***Light Exposure***: Get morning sunlight as soon as possible after arrival to reset your internal clock.

Nutrition for Focus and Mood

Good nutrition is for your muscles, brain chemistry, and emotional stability. The right foods at the correct times can boost concentration, prevent crashes, and help keep your mood steady during long training days or stressful competitions.

Simple Pre- and Post-Practice Snacks

Pre-Practice (1 – 2 hours before)	
Goal: Quick energy and steady blood sugar	
Fruit + Protein Combo	*Ex:* *1 banana/ apple* *1 to 2 tbsp peanut butter/ almond butter* *Handful of nuts*

Whole-Grain Energy Base	*1 slice whole-grain toast/ rice cake*
	1 boiled egg/ slice of turkey
	Drizzle of honey or fruit
Dairy Power-Up	*1 cup Greek yogurt/ cottage cheese*
	Berries/ granola
	A small handful of pumpkin seeds
Liquid fuel (if short on time)	*1 smoothie (milk/ almond milk + banana + oats + scoop of protein powder/ peanut butter)*
On-the-Go Bar Combo	*1 oat/ granola bar (check for low added sugar)*
	Small piece of fruit (orange/ apple/ dried dates)

Post-Practice (within 45 minutes)
Goal: Rebuild and rehydrate

Classic Recovery Shake	*Chocolate milk/ protein shake (20–25g protein)*
	1 banana/ handful of berries
Simple Protein + Carb Plate	*Turkey/ chicken wrap*
	Piece of fruit

	Water or electrolyte drink
Build-a-Bowl	*Rice/ quinoa base* *Lean protein (chicken/ tofu/ tuna)* *Veggies and olive oil drizzle*
Yogurt Bowl Recovery	*Greek yogurt + granola + sliced fruit* *Water or a low-sugar sports drink*
Breakfast-for-Dinner Option	*2 eggs + whole-grain toast* *Orange juice/ fruit smoothie*

Consistency beats perfection. Eating well 80% of the time makes a bigger difference than obsessing over "perfect" meals.

Hydration Rules of Thumb

Dehydration can tank performance faster than fatigue or soreness. Even a 2% drop in body water can affect focus and mood.

- Start the day with a full glass of water.
- **Before Practice:** Drink water until your urine is pale yellow.
- **During:** Sip throughout practice, every 15 to 20 minutes (don't wait until you're thirsty and don't chug all at once).
- After practice, aim for two to three cups (about 500 to 750 ml) of fluids for every pound of sweat lost.

Signs of Poor Fueling or Hydration

- ☐ Constant fatigue or irritability.
- ☐ Headaches or dizziness.
- ☐ Cramping more often than usual.
- ☐ Difficulty focusing during practice or games.

When to Refer to a Nutritionist

If you're losing excessive energy, struggling with recovery, or dealing with recurring injuries, it's time to get professional help.

A sports nutritionist can:

- Create a personalized diet plan for your training schedule.
- Address allergies or deficiencies (e.g., iron, vitamin D).
- Help manage eating habits around performance anxiety or travel.
- Keep your relationship with fuel and food healthy and stable.

Remember: your meals are part of your training plan, *not* an afterthought.

Movement for Regulation

The way you move shapes your mind as much as your muscles. That is why you need to learn how to use movement intentionally to manage emotions and mindset.

Micro-Mobility and Breath Circuits

A 'micro-mobility circuit' is a three to five-minute flow you can do anywhere (before class, in your room, before practice) to wake up your body and brain.

Energizing Circuit (a.m. or pre-practice):

- Jumping jacks (30 sec)
- Arm circles (30 sec)
- Hip openers (30 sec)
- Controlled breathing: 3 quick inhales, three slow exhales (3 rounds)

Calming Circuit (p.m. or post-game):

- Cat-cow stretch (1 min)
- Forward fold (30 sec)
- Deep squat hold (30 sec)
- Box breathing: In 4, hold 4, out 4, hold 4 (2 to 3 min)

Active Recovery and Cross-Training

Rest days aren't about 'doing nothing.' They're about **moving with intention.** Light activities like swimming (if you're not a competitive swimmer, of course), yoga, or biking keep blood flowing and reduce stiffness. Cross-training also helps prevent overuse injuries.

Here's an example of a weekly schedule:

- *Mon to Fri*: Sport-specific training.
- *Sat*: Light cross-training (bike, swim, or stretch).
- *Sun*: Full rest or mindfulness session.

Using Movement to Interrupt Negative Thought Spirals

Everyone faces mental slumps, be it frustration after a mistake, anxiety before a competition, or burnout mid-season. When negative thoughts spiral, if words aren't doing what they need to, another tool you can use is **motion.**

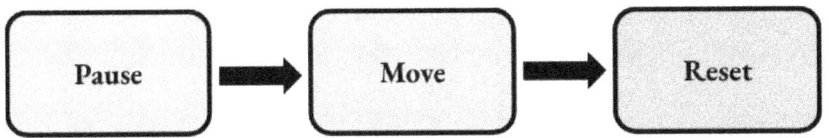

If you catch yourself overthinking:

1. *Pause:* Step away from what you're doing for 30 seconds.
2. *Move:* Do 10 push-ups, a wall sit, jumping jacks, or a slow-breathing walk.
3. *Reset*: Ask, "What's one small action I can take right now?"

Movement resets your nervous system, helping your brain shift from stress, anxious, or panic mode to action mode.

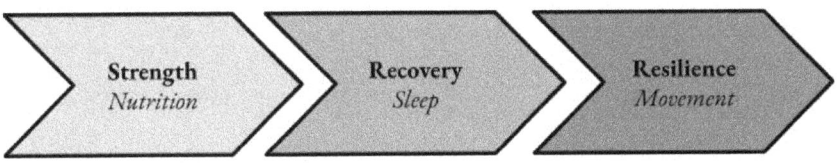

Tech, Measurement, and Boundaries

Technology can be both your best training buddy *and* your biggest distraction. From apps that track your sleep to smartwatches that measure your heart rate, there's no shortage of gadgets promising to make you stronger. However, tech is only valid when you stay in charge of it, not the other way around.

Helpful Tech and What to Avoid

Low-cost trackers (like Fitbit, Whoop, or even certain phone apps) can be great tools to learn about your body's rhythms. They can tell you things like how many hours you slept, your resting heart rate, and how long you were in deep sleep. If your tracker helps you notice patterns (like "I sleep better when I stop scrolling before bed.") that's a win.

There are also nutrition and hydration apps that work well for tracking food and water intake.

The problems emerge when people obsess over the numbers. Some athletes wake up and check their sleep score before checking how they *feel*. That can actually lead to anxiety and make you perform worse. If you've slept "only" seven hours but feel sharp and ready, trust your body. Recovery isn't measured perfectly by tech, but experienced through your energy.

In other words, use the data as a *guide*, not a *judge*.

Coaches and parents can help by turning the numbers into stories. Replace *"Your sleep score dropped by 10%,"* with *"You seemed sharper after those early nights this week. What changed?"* This helps connect data to real-world cause-and-effect.

There's also a dark side to tech: **banned or unsafe practices**. Be cautious of any app or wearable that asks for too much personal info (banking info, detailed health stats, etc.), promotes "bio-hacks" that sound extreme, or pressures you to share data publicly. Always do privacy checks before linking devices to social accounts or team dashboards. Your data belongs to *you*.

If you're under 18, make sure what is shared is reviewed by a parent or guardian.

Quick Tech Filter

- Use for awareness, learning, and progress.
- Avoid using it for comparison or punishment.
- Never share private data or use "hacks" that skip proper rest and nutrition.

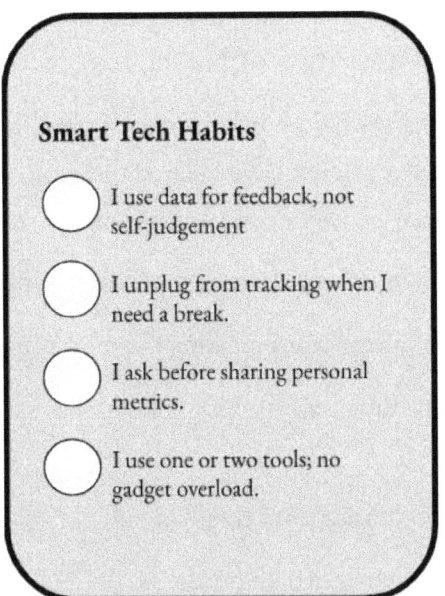

Digital Hygiene and Attention Management

Rule #1: No screens 60 minutes before bed

Even brief exposure to blue light delays your sleep cycle, which can disrupt recovery, focus, and muscle repair.

One hour before bed, put your phone across the room. Use that last hour for stretching, journaling, or visualization instead.

Rule #2: Protect your focus windows

During homework, workouts, or study sessions, keep your phone out of reach or in silent mode. Constant notifications can train your brain to crave micro-distractions, which weaken your ability to stay in the zone.

You can use simple tools to help. Some athletes put their phones in alarmed lock boxes (timed containers that don't open until your session is done). Others use parental timers or focus apps (Focus/ Freedom/

Stay Focused) that limit screen time during key hours or for certain apps. What matters is not really the tool, but more so controlling the habit.

Parents and coaches should be part of this system, too. Their mission isn't to take tech away (which is virtually impossible nowadays), but to share boundaries that protect everyone's growth and effort.

Coaches might have an agreement with their athletes:

- No phones during team meetings or warm-ups.
- Wind-down time after night games before checking social media.
- No scrolling during team travel meals.
- Mutual respect for offline hours.

At home, parents can model the same behavior. If their phone is off during dinner or bedtime, it's easier for teens to do the same. You're all training the same discipline: attention control.

Ethical Considerations with Data

With great power, as we all know, comes great responsibility. The ethical use of data is both a legal *and* a respect rule.

If you're a minor (under 18), any tracking or data collection should always come with **informed consent**.

That means you and your parents should know:

- What data is being collected (like heart rate or sleep time)?
- Who has access (coaches, trainers, or apps).
- How it will be used (for training adjustments, not competition rankings).

Transparency is everything. Coaches and schools should clearly explain data policies and ensure athletes can ask questions. No one should feel pressured to share private info just to stay on the team.

You can always say no to sharing any particular info.

One major boundary: no public leaderboards or comparisons without consent.

It might sound fun to compare step counts or sleep hours, but this can quickly turn toxic. Imagine being shamed for "only" sleeping six hours or missing recovery goals because of stress at home. Data should inform, not embarrass.

If you're ever unsure, ask these three questions before sharing:

1. *"Do I understand what's being collected?"*
2. *"Do I know who can see it?"*
3. *"Will it help me grow, not stress me out?"*

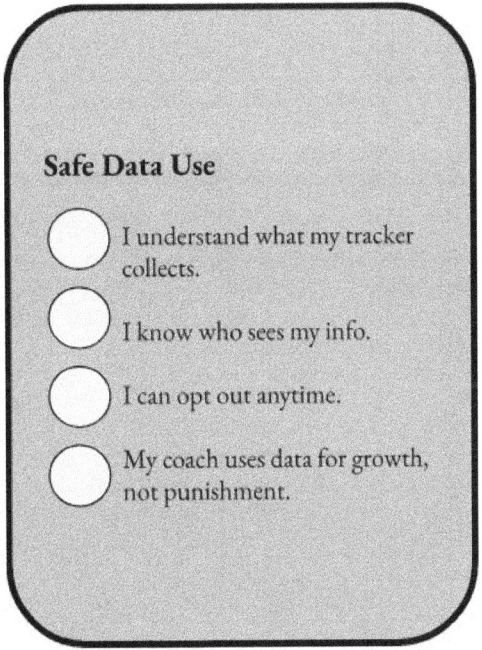

When data is used ethically, it reflects patterns you can learn from, not ones that judge or pressure. Coaches can model this by using language focused on learning:

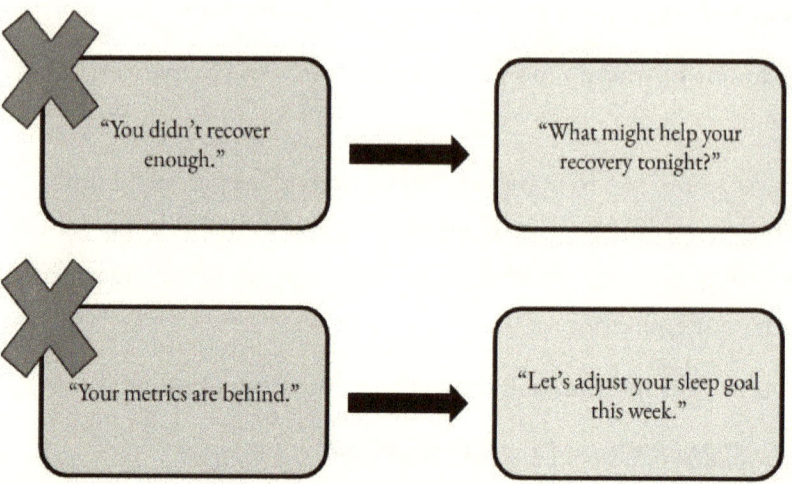

Just like with other goals and weekly cycles from previous chapters, try to set three 'tech' goals for yourself every 3-week cycle (along with your other motivation and habit goals).

	3-Week Tech Boundary Challenge	
Week	Focus Goal	Habit Check
1	Ex: No phone 30 mins before bed. (Daily)	○○○○○○○
2	Phone-free during workouts. (Daily)	○○○○○○○
3	Ask for data transparency (coach/parent).	Done? ☐

In the bigger picture, these habits teach life skills beyond sports. Learning how to build habits, manage your sleep and nutrition, control your attention, protect your data, and maintain digital balance all help you perform better, not only in games, but also in school, relationships, and future jobs.

Now, it's time to move on to the final pillar of mental toughness: decision-making intelligence. You've honed your mindset and your body, so it's time to sharpen your thinking skills through perception training, pressure labs, and creative outlets.

Key Takeaways

- High performance is about building systems and habits that sustain excellence through your environment, micro-habits, and recovery.
- Sleep, nutrition, and movement are the foundations on which everything is built: sleep is where you grow, food is how you think, and movement is how you feel. Being consistent with small daily wins (better sleep tonight, a snack before training, a 5-minute stretch) compounds into long-term success.
- When you combine tech tools with smart boundaries, you get a sharper focus, deeper recovery, and a stronger sense of control over your athletic journey.

Champion Mantra:

"You can't outperform poor recovery; resting builds the mind."

Chapter 7: Decision Making and Game Intelligence

All kinds of games, routines, and sports competitions sometimes feel like everything's happening "too fast." Every athlete, at some point, has felt the speed of an event was overwhelming, leading them to react a second too late, make a rushed pass, or miss an open teammate.

The solution to this isn't necessarily just moving faster, but *seeing* faster. Training your brain to pick up patterns before anyone else even realizes what's happening, strengthening your perception and anticipation.

Ecological dynamics research explains this perfectly: your brain and body learn through **interaction with the environment**. That means the best way to sharpen your game sense isn't just memorizing plays or watching highlight reels (though visual skill acquisition is still helpful); it's through realistic, constraint-based training that mirrors the chaos of real competition.

Perception and Anticipation Training

Davids et al., in their book *Dynamics of Skill Acquisition*, sum up the three factors performers (particularly athletes) need to do well:

1) Ensure they contact an object or surface in the environment at the appropriate moment.

2) Ensure contact at the intended velocity and force.

3) Ensure contact at an intended spatial orientation.

"To satisfy these task constraints, performers need access to quality information to support their actions." (Davids et al., 2008, p.56)

This might seem like a lot of things you *need* to do in that split second, but the truth is, you have all the information to carry this out.

You just need to see it.

Pattern Recognition Drills

In every sport, patterns drive performance. A point guard recognizes defensive rotations before the trap forms. A striker reads the defender's hips before making a run. A goalkeeper catches the slightest shift that signals a shot. These split-second recognitions are **trained perceptions** that, over time, evolve into **instincts**.

Step 1: Start with video cue-spotting progressions

1. Choose short clips from real games or events in your sport.
2. Pause them right before key moments (the pass, the tackle, the shot, the jump, the flip, etc.).
3. Now, ask: "What happens next?" Try to identify which **cues** give it away (body angle, hand position, foot pressure, speed of approach).

Over time, shorten the clip duration and the pause time until you're spotting cues at full speed. This kind of video training builds the link between what your eyes see and how your body reacts.

Step 2: Then, move to representative design tasks

This means setting up drills that *look* and *feel* like the actual game environment. Davids et al. emphasize that **representative design** is vital; your drills must contain the same perception-action couplings as real play. For example, instead of static passing drills, add defenders who shift unpredictably or teammates who move through real passing lanes.

The goal is to train your perception in the context of **live affordances**: the opportunities for action that emerge naturally in gameplay.

Step 3: Finally, check for transfer

Drills only matter if they transfer into actual games. During scrimmages, track whether the patterns you practiced appear in play, and whether you recognize them earlier than before.

You might even journal/note down your reals:

- *"I saw the defender step early this time."*
- *"I noticed the opening before the cut."*

This reflection closes the loop between perception training and live decision-making.

Pattern recognition isn't about seeing passively; it's about **interpreting**. The more patterns you expose yourself to, the less the game surprises you.

Timing, Tempo, and Rhythm Training

Game intelligence = rhythm awareness.

Every play or sequence has a pulse: the tempo of a fast break, the beat of a swimming stroke, the micro-rhythm of passing sequences. Great athletes are almost always in sync with the game's rhythm.

Tempo Manipulation Drills

For example, in basketball or soccer, run sequences where the coach or captain randomly calls out "slow," "normal," or "fast" to force the team to adapt their tempo instantly. The goal is to maintain decision quality under changing speeds. Your mind learns to anticipate at multiple tempos, strengthening adaptability.

In tennis, baseball, or volleyball, you can do the same with **timing windows**. Practice reacting to serves or throws at varying speeds or trajectories. As your perception adjusts, your body becomes better at **tuning** its response.

Slow-Motion Reps to Refine Timing Errors

Sometimes, slowing down helps you feel the correct sequence. Move through plays in exaggerated slow motion, focusing on the moment of decision (this is especially helpful in sports that don't necessarily rely on external speeds, but skill sequences like swimming and gymnastics). When do you *see* the cue? When do you *decide*? When do you *act*? The delay between perception and action is called your **decision latency window**. The shorter it gets, the better your anticipation.

You can measure this informally: film a practice, and note how long it takes you to respond to an event. Are you reading early enough to act without rushing? Controlling that tempo trains anticipation. By stretching and compressing the rhythm of play, you teach your brain to predict rather than react.

Micro Playbooks and Heuristics

When you're in the middle of a game or event, there's no time for overthinking. That's where **heuristics** (mental shortcuts) come in. These are simple 'if X then Y' rules that help you make fast decisions under pressure—sort of like a quick access button.

Build micro playbooks for your position.

These should be one-page summaries of the most common game situations you face. You'll find some examples below for different sports and positions (non-exhaustive lists of all possible 'if X then Y' plays).

You can build these from your own film review. Identify three or four scenarios that repeat every game, and define your best response. Keep it simple and visual, something you can glance at before practice or games.

Pre-game scripts for common game states

Create scripts that promote mental clarity (also using the 'If X then Y' template). These scripts prevent emotional overreactions and keep your decision-making aligned with team objectives, not impulses. For example,

> *"If we're down early, focus on tempo control. If we're up late, slow transitions and protect possession."*

Rehearse heuristics in short team blocks.

Instead of long tactical meetings, run micro-sessions where each player executes their heuristics at game speed. Coaches can also design 'constraint games' that force specific scenarios; for instance, by stating every drill from a turnover or a 3-on-2 situation. The point isn't to *memorize* the playbook, but to train the perception-decision link under **authentic pressure**.

This is what ecological dynamics research terms **exploring the landscape of affordances**: the more you train in context, the richer your perception of opportunities becomes. Eventually, these heuristics move from conscious rules to automatic responses, freeing your mind to focus on creativity and adaptability.

The Decision-Making Loop

See Patterns	Feel Tempo	Act Instinctively
Train with realistic cues	*Adjust rhythm and timing*	*Apply heuristics under pressure*

This loop repeats every time you play. The more realistic your practice environment, the more automatic your decision-making becomes. In ecological dynamics terms, you're improving **attunement**: the ability to detect the most useful information in your environment and act on it without delay.

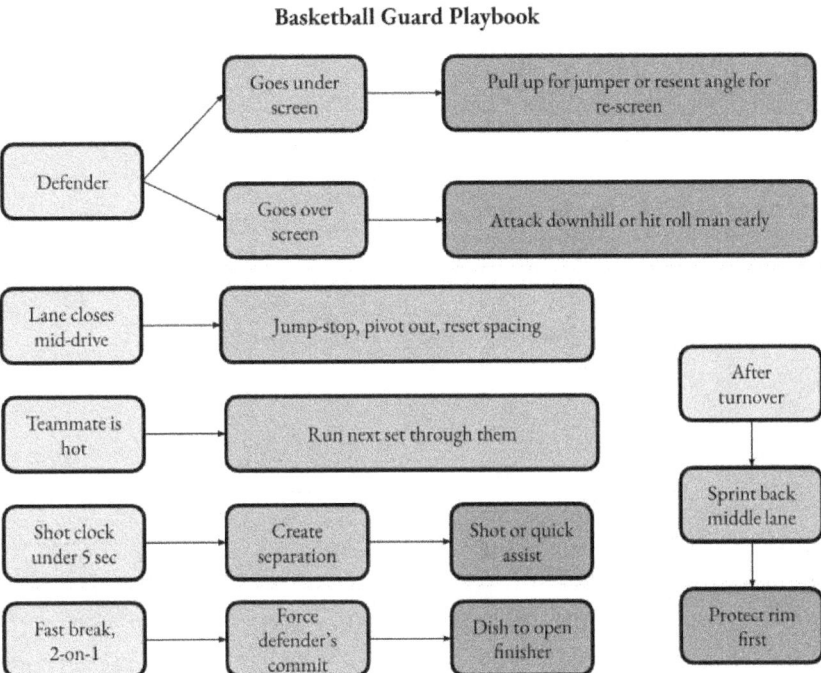

Basketball Guard Playbook

Soccer Midfielder Playbook

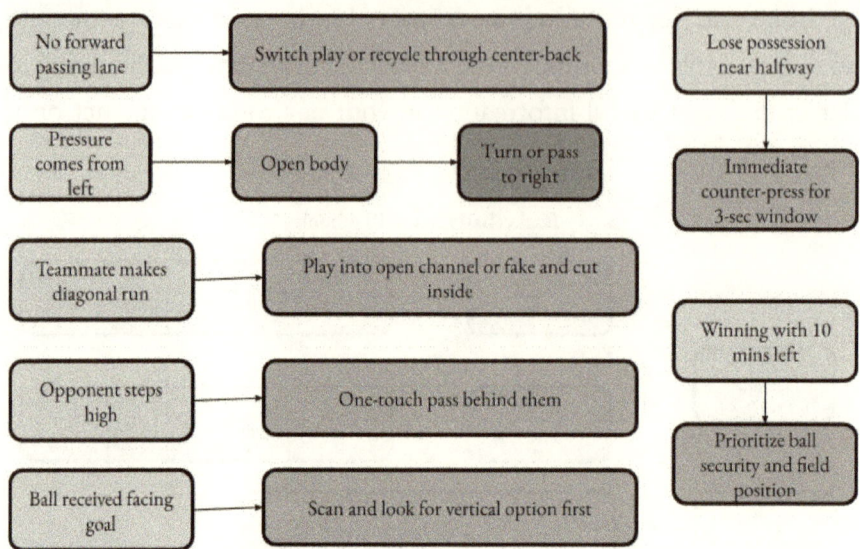

Football Quarterback Playbook

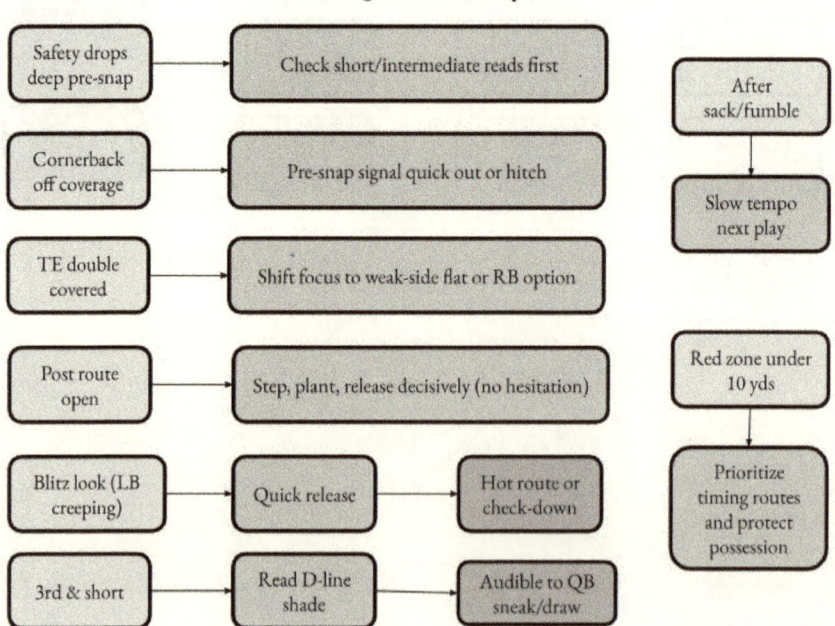

Young Athletes' Blueprint for Mental Toughness

Baseball Batter Playbook

- Fastball inside → Turn hips, dive to pull gap
- Pitcher repeats sequence → Anticipate pattern → Adjust stance accordingly
- Ahead in count → Sit on your pitch and swing aggressively
- Behind in count → Shorten swing, protect plate
- Off-speed pitch mid-flight → Delay, keep weight back, go opposite field
- Two outs, full count → Swing only if it's clearly in the zone
- Fielders shifted right → Aim to opposite field

Volleyball Setter Playbook

- Middle blocker commits early → Set outside fast
- Opposite side hitter cold → Run quicks or back sets to vary attack
- Pass too tight to net → Dump set or push high outside
- Blockers slow to reset → Tempo quick set to middle
- Defense deep → Tip short or call for roll shot
- Serve receive off target → Communicate emergency set option
- Front-row mismatch → Exploit height or attack seam

Hockey Defensemen Playbook

If...	Then...
Forward attacking with speed	Close gap early, angle outside
Puck dumped into corner	Body first, stick second → Seal boards
Breakout under pressure	Off boards or D-to-D for relief
Weak-side winger open	Hard cross-ice pass only if safe lane
Opponent cycles behind net	Communicate switch early
Lost puck battle	Recover middle ice first
Penalty kill	Keep stick in lane, force play wide

Tennis Player Playbook

If...	Then...
Opponent deep behind baseline	Drop shot or short angle
Opponent hits short ball	Attack and approach net
Opponent slicing often	Step in, take ball early
You're late on returns	Back up half step to buy time
Long rally developing	Change height or spin to break rhythm
Down break point	High-percentage serve to body
Up 40–0	Try aggressive variation

Training for Transfer and Pressure

In real games, no two situations are the same. The best athletes are the ones who can *adapt*. That's the essence of a **constraint-led approach**.

Instead of drilling the same movement 100 times, training is designed to shape your decisions through realistic constraints; researchers call this **constraint-based training**.

Constraint-Led Training for Adaptive Choices

Constraints come in three types:

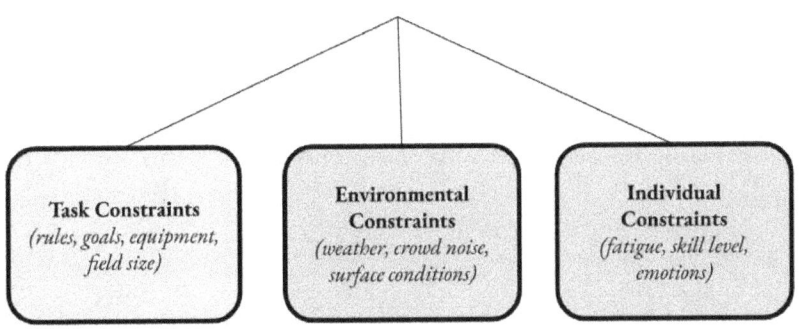

By adjusting these, coaches can make you think, perceive, and react in ways that transfer directly to competition.

For example, if a coach shrinks the playing area in a soccer drill, you're forced to make quicker passes and scan faster. If they give you only two touches before passing, your brain learns to anticipate earlier. If a defender starts slightly behind you each rep, you must adapt your timing to win the race to the ball. These are all **designed constraints** that teach adaptive decision-making under realistic conditions.

The goal isn't to make drills difficult just for the sake of being "difficult." They're *shaping intelligent behavior*. When the constraint fits the learning goal, your brain finds new ways to succeed. Your playbook of experiences is going to keep expanding, reducing decision-time, and increasing what sport psychologists call **functional variability**.

Progression Rules

Coaches should scale challenges *safely*. If you're a beginner, too many constraints can cause confusion, demotivation, or even poor form. It's best to start with *manageable limits*, like slightly less time or a smaller space. Then, layer difficulty as your confidence grows. **Safety scaling** ensures you stay in what psychologists call the **challenge zone**: not too easy, not too overwhelming. This keeps your nervous system engaged while reducing the risk of injury or burnout.

Coach Prompts

Coaches may love telling you *what* to do, but that can actually be a hindrance in constraints-led training.

The best coaches ask questions that make you explore the options yourself:

- *"What did you see before you passed?"*
- *"How could you create more time in the next play?"*
- *"What changed when space got smaller?"*
- *"Where was your focus when the play opened up?"*
- *"What did the defender's body tell you?"*
- *"How did the time limit change your decision?"*
- *"What cues helped you spot that opportunity?"*
- *"How early did you pick up that pattern?"*

Pressure Lab and Controlled Exposure

Even if your technique is perfect in training, pressure can make everything fall apart. Your heart rate spikes, your hands shake, and your vision narrows. That's why top performers practice under pressure.

A 'pressure lab' isn't some fancy, expensive facility; it's just your mindset and the structure you build into regular practice. The idea is to simulate the emotions and sensations of real competition in controlled, progressive ways:

- Crowd sounds blasting through a speaker during free throws.
- Countdown clocks that cut reaction time in half.
- Scoreboard stress, like needing one point to win.

These setups activate your stress response (adrenaline, heart rate, and focus shifts) while remaining safe and coach-controlled. The goal is to train your body to *feel pressure* and *stay functional*.

You can start with short exposures, maybe one or two minutes, followed by an immediate debrief. This debrief is where you learn and reflect, taking a few minutes with your coach or teammate to answer:

- *"What did I feel?"*
- *"What helped me stay calm?"*
- *"What threw me off?"*

This reflection helps you process the experience and adapt faster next time.

Coaches can also track physiological markers during these drills, such as heart rate, breathing rhythm, and simple signs like how quickly you recover between reps. Then, you'll be able to see whether your stress responses become smoother and more efficient.

To take it further, you can combine constraint-led drills with pressure training. For instance, shorten the field (constraint) while adding a time limit and crowd noise (pressure). The result will be your brain learning to adapt intelligently while under stress.

Rapid Reflection Loops

The final piece in training for transfer is reflection. But let's avoid the long, boring kind. All you need is 60 seconds to lock in learning while your brain is still buzzing from action.

After each high-intensity or high-pressure rep, pause and run this mental script:

Reflection Loop

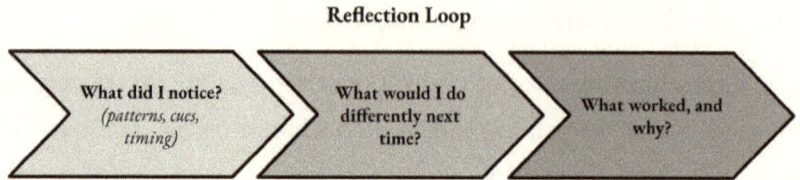

These questions shift your focus from outcome ("Did I score?") to process ("What helped me make that read?") —the ideology that we deemed essential in the previous chapter.

When players take ownership of this loop, they start to drive their own development. Coaches are no longer controlling the session; they are **facilitating autonomy** (one of the key tenets of intrinsic motivation). The goal is to create **micro-adjustments**: minor tweaks in perception, timing, or body language that make a big difference. Maybe you realize you hold your breath before a shot or stop scanning when tired. Catching these patterns early lets you adjust on the fly.

According to ecological dynamics, learning is an **emergent process**: you don't "install" new skills like apps; you *self-organize* them through exploration and feedback.

To close the reflection loop, record and repeat successful adaptations. Spot what strategies work and what you tend to miss. If something works (a new move, a calmer breathing rhythm, a more brilliant passing read), *log it*. Then, recreate it in the next session under slightly more challenging constraints or pressure.

All of this solidifies your performance system.

Performance System

Creativity and Problem-Solving

Now that you've trained how to recognize the patterns, make quick decisions, and adapt under pressure, it's time to find creative solutions to the problems that come your way. Constraints appear again here because this is where you explore solutions within them, setting up challenges that push you to think laterally.

In other words, you're not just following the "standard" play, but inventing new ones on the spot.

Lateral Thinking and Improvisation Games

Lateral thinking means looking at a problem from a new angle. It's what happens when you stop trying to find the "right" answer and start searching for *different* ones.

When the passing lane's blocked, you spin the other way.

When a defender overplays, you change pace.

You can train this skill through improvisation games:

Cross-Sport Games

Try borrowing tasks from other sports. For example, a soccer player might run a drill that mimics a basketball's fast-ball movement and spacing. A basketball player might try "soccer passing" rules that ban dribbling, forcing creative off-ball movement. These cross-sport tasks shape your habits and make your brain flexible.

Constraint Switches

You're probably tired of seeing the word 'constraints,' but they're just super helpful.

Change one small rule every few minutes (again, like limiting touches, shrinking space, or reversing dominant hand/foot use). The goal isn't to perfect the new version, but to adapt quickly and discover new movement solutions.

Improvisation Bursts

Add surprise elements during scrimmages, like a random countdown, an unexpected extra teammate, or a bonus point for creative plays. These tweaks create the "chaos" that mirrors real game pressure and fuels innovation.

In the end, reward the novelty that works. Coaches and teammates should recognize how a move was discovered, regardless of whether it *succeeded* or not. When a player tries something new, even if it doesn't entirely work, it deserves recognition for creativity.

After these sessions, a debrief helps clarify progress.

Ask questions like:

- *"What made that move possible?"*
- *"What cues did you notice that helped you decide?"*
- *"How could that idea transfer to a real game?"*

By talking it through, you start to connect creative exploration with real-time decision-making. You're teaching your brain to **generalize creativity**, to bring that same problem-solving mindset to every game situation.

Role Rotation and Mixed-Age Scrimmages

One of the biggest creative boosters is seeing the game from a new perspective, in steps of **role rotation**. By swapping positions, even temporarily, you deepen your understanding of the whole system.

For example, if you're a striker in soccer, try playing as a defender for a few games or scrimmages. You'll start noticing what defenders look for, how they track runs, and where the blind spots are. Next time you switch back, you'll have better timing, sharper deception, and more empathy for your teammates. In ecological terms, you're expanding your **perceptual-motor landscape**: building a richer library of cues that guide future actions (Davids et al., 2008, p.82-3).

Coaches can design sessions where athletes rotate every few minutes or after every drill, ultimately stretching their perception. Your brain constantly remaps how space, timing, and affordances change with perspective, and your adaptability skyrockets.

Mixed-age scrimmages take this idea even further. Younger athletes benefit from watching and copying older players' pacing, communication, and positioning. Meanwhile, older players improve their adaptability by adjusting their speed and strategies to match different ability levels. It's a win-win situation.

Imagine a 14-year-old playing with 17-year-olds: they'll learn faster, make better decisions, and develop sharper spatial awareness. But when older players scrimmage with younger ones, they're challenged to use timing, angles, and leadership rather than raw power. This variety of experiences accelerates skill acquisition by continually reshaping the performer-environment relationship.

Of course, safety and scaling apply here as well. When mixing ages or rotating roles, coaches should tweak the space, contact rules, or even ball size so everyone can play confidently.

Some examples include:

- Reducing contact intensity in mixed-age games.
- Using smaller fields or lighter balls for younger athletes.
- Pairing more experienced players as mentors during role rotations.

The goal is to maintain the challenge without risking injury or overwhelming the less experienced players.

Simple Analytics for Decision Coaching

Numbers can be helpful, but they should never take over. They are feedback, *not* a scoreboard. What matters is how well your decisions matched the situation.

Rather than tracking hundreds of stats, focus on a few meaningful ones:

- *Decision Outcomes*: Did your choice create an advantage (space, possession, shot opportunity, etc.)?
- *Turnovers*: Were they caused by poor perception, slow timing, or risky creativity worth trying?
- *Choice Quality*: Did you recognize the best option available, even if the execution is missed?

Keep these numbers "light," that is, not judgmental, but learning patterns. You'll see trends: maybe your decisions improve under pressure, or perhaps you rush plays in specific zones. Now, use that data.

Just like with all the training we did throughout this book, coaches should translate the numbers into stories. "You had four turnovers" becomes "Two of those were creative attempts that almost worked. Let's adjust your spacing so they succeed next time." This way, analytics becomes a **growth tool**, helping athletes link decisions to context.

The danger is **over-quantifying:** drowning athletes in charts or making them fear mistakes. As soon as athletes start chasing stats, they stop experimenting.

If you're self-tracking or using an app, keep these principles in mind:

- Focus on trends, not single performances.
- Reflect on what the numbers *mean* for your awareness and adaptability.
- Always connect data to learning steps: "What can I tweak next practice?"

Ultimately, behavior emerges from the interaction between player, task, and environment. Numbers simply highlight which interactions need refining.

Decision-making and game intelligence aren't about flashy tricks or wild risks; they're about adaptability, confidence, and problem-solving under pressure. You train this ability to read situations, reduce decision fatigue, turn actions into instinct, experiment with different contexts, and evolve as *thinkers* and players.

In the final chapter, we're going to address the difficulties every athlete faces with adversity and setbacks, as well as the realities of injuries from a mental perspective. You'll learn what psychological first aid entails, what's involved in staged rehab, and the growth that emerges from comebacks.

Key Takeaways

- Game intelligence is shaped through experience, training your eyes, developing rhythm, and using heuristics in environments that mirror real play so your brain can predict what comes next.

- Training in pressure resilience leads to more thoughtful decision-making by helping people adapt to unpredictable situations, build emotional control and composure under stress, lock in lessons, and promote autonomy.

- Playful exploration that involves cross-sport training, role rotations, and mixed-age scrimmages is how creativity and skills grow. Good decisions, even if they don't pan out, are just as helpful as drills.

Champion Mantra:

"Faster decisions come from better perception. So, practice what your eyes should see."

Chapter 8: Adversity, Injury, and the Comeback Mindset

People love comeback stories. They get excited over the moment an athlete returns after months away, stronger and sharper than before. What most people don't realize, though, is that the *real* comeback starts long before the first practice back.

It begins on day one of the injury.

In the athlete's mindset. In their routines. In their support networks.

Injury is a given risk in sports. Even the most careful and best-equipped athletes can sometimes get injured in the fast-paced and high-stakes world of athletics. While coaches and trainers often teach players how *not* to get injured, just as important is teaching players about the psychological side of injury, from the first emotional crash to the rebuilding phase.

It's time to turn setbacks into comebacks.

Psychological First Aid and Inclusion

According to Weinberg and Gould (2019), injured athletes' responses fall into three categories that they often go through as the injured state progresses:

1. Injury-relevant information processing.
2. Emotional upheaval and reactive behavior.

3. Positive outlook and coping.

(Weinberg & Gould, 2019, p.599).

It's up to coaches, families, trainers, and players themselves to deal with each stage in a mentally healthy way.

Day-One Scripts and Containment

We start with stage one: *the injury.*

When an athlete gets injured, emotions often swing between panic, denial, depression, and fear of being left behind. Coaches, parents, and teammates can make or break that moment. Research in rehab psychology emphasizes the importance of **containment**: creating a safe, calm environment where the injured person feels seen, understood, and stable.

Calm and validating language can help coaches or parents respond without making things worse:

- *"This sucks, and it's okay to feel frustrated. We're going to take this one step at a time."*
- *"You're still part of the team. We'll figure out how you can stay involved during recovery."*
- *"We'll handle the medical side, but for now let's focus on what you can control today."*

These short and grounded phrases communicate empathy and structure. The first 24 hours should focus on reducing chaos and restoring predictability. The athlete needs *clear next steps*: when to see the doctor, what to expect in the next few days, and how communication will flow among the coach, parent, and medical professionals. Research also shows that when athletes *understand* the injury from a medical and physiological perspective, it helps reduce the uncertainty surrounding the situation.

Immediate Routine Restoration

Rehab psychologists call this the **stability anchor**. Even if training stops, you should try to keep small elements of your normal rhythm: attending team meetings, doing modified drills, journaling progress, and helping set up practice equipment. These routines lower anxiety and prevent spiraling into burnout or identity loss.

Referral Checkpoints

Coaches should have a simple checklist:

- Medical evaluation complete
- Emotional status noted (shock, frustration, withdrawal)
- Family or counselor referral offered if distress is high
- Follow-up communication plan made

Documentation makes recovery structured and visible; not just physical rehab, but mental stability tracking too. Simply knowing that there's a plan can restore your confidence and sense of control.

Preserve Identity and Belonging

One of the most significant risks after injury is **identity loss**: when athletes begin to believe that without their sport, they're no one. This is a substantial trigger for depression, disengagement, and even quitting the sport altogether. The way to prevent this is *inclusion*: keeping injured players actively involved in team life.

Coaches can assign non-physical roles that maintain purpose and connection.

For example:

- *Analyst*: Review video footage and share notes with teammates.
- *Mentor*: Support younger players during drills or strategy sessions.
- *Planner*: Help design warm-ups or tactical adjustments.
- *Scout*: Observe opponents and identify tendencies.

Thus, 'bench time' becomes transformed into 'growth time.' You continue to contribute value, which keeps your motivation alive and identity intact.

Micro-tasks to Preserve Agency

When you're injured, often the most significant mental challenge is losing control. So, creating tasks that let athletes *do* something each day is vital:

- Track recovery exercises.
- Schedule rehab sessions.
- Design game notes.
- Set mini-goals, like "increase motion by 5% this week."

Even small wins can reinforce your self-efficacy after injury.

Family Inclusion Plans

These are usually overlooked. Families often feel unsure about how to help, wondering whether to push, comfort, or back off. Creating a recovery communication plan helps everyone stay aligned. Plus, research has shown that athletes with a larger social support network recover mentally faster and use more positive coping mechanisms.

This plan could include:

- A shared online calendar for appointments and rehab tasks.

- Weekly 'check-in dinner' where the athlete shares progress and emotions.
- Parents agree to focus conversations on **effort and mood**, not just timelines.

Structured Emotional Processing

Injury recovery is rarely linear. It's emotional and *deeply* personal. Rehab psychology outlines a stage map, similar to grief cycles, guiding both athletes and supporters.

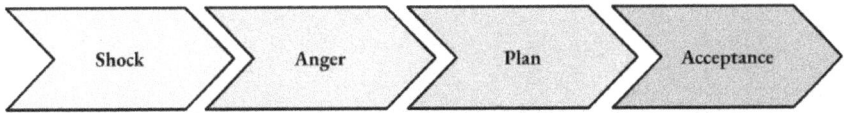

Injury-Recovery Stage Map

Stage 1: Shock

Right after the injury, athletes often feel numb or disoriented. The best activity here is **grounding**: focusing on breathing, the environment, and the immediate next steps. A simple technique is the 'Five Senses Reset':

Name 5 things you can see:

4 you can touch,

3 you can hear,

2 you can smell,

1 you can taste.

This calms the nervous system and reduces panic.

Stage 2: Anger

Once reality sets in, frustration is often the next step. This could be anger at the situation, coaches, teammates, or even yourself. The key is to *channel it* rather than suppress it.

For example:

- Write an uncensored journal entry: "This is unfair because…"
- Then, transform that list into "What I still control…" to pivot towards action.

This process reclaims agency and reduces helplessness.

Stage 3: Plan

This is the turning point. You begin to visualize progress and set structured goals. Coaches and physios can help design a tiered comeback map:

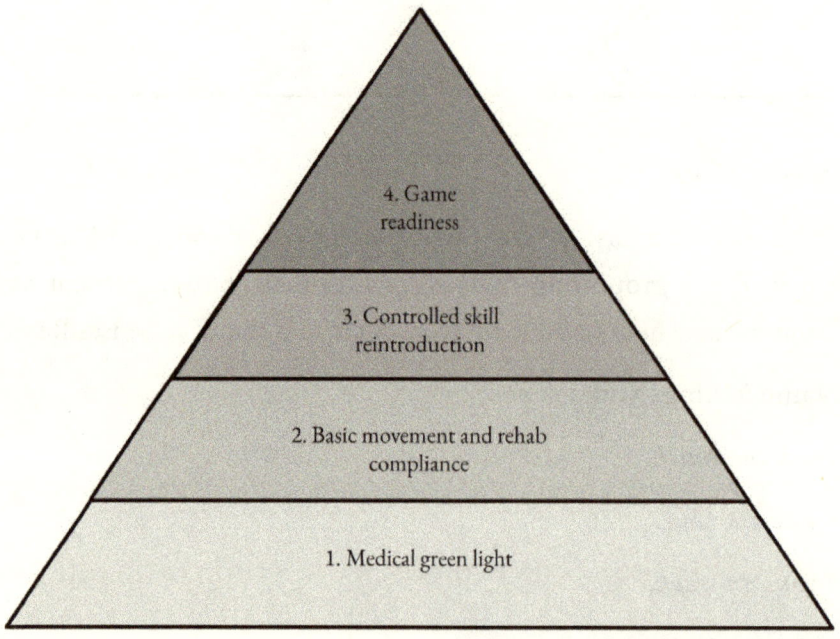

Seeing this roadmap turns recovery from a waiting game into a *challenge*.

Stage 4: Acceptance

Acceptance isn't giving up; it's focusing entirely on the process rather than the pain. You can deepen your reflection here through guided prompts like:

- *"What has this injury taught me about patience or resilience?"*
- *"What parts of me have grown while I couldn't compete?"*
- *"How can I support others going through similar setbacks?"*

Turning your experience into wisdom is a vital part of long-term mental toughness.

Team Rituals to Re-Welcome Returning Athletes

When the comeback begins, the return to play can be just as emotionally charged as the injury itself. Teammates may not know how to react. Should they go easy on you? Cheer you on extra hard? Or act totally normal?

In this case, coaches can design re-entry rituals that make the transition smoother and meaningful:

- A short 'welcome-back circle' where teammates share one appreciation or lesson learned from the athlete's recovery.
- A symbolic act: the athlete reclaiming their jersey or leading the team in warm-ups again.
- A shared reflection session where the team discusses what resilience looks like in their culture.

Rehab Psychology and Return Protocols

Despite all the positivity coaches and teams can bring, at the end of the day, returning to sport can be a very challenging time for many reasons:

- Anxiety over re-injury
- Performance anxiety
- Worried about meeting expectations
- Decreased physical self-efficacy

- Uncertainty over reaching pre-injury levels

There are plenty of protocols and strategies that can help athletes through the rehab process.

Staged Goal Setting and Celebration

Healing bones and muscles is one thing; rebuilding confidence, discipline, and belief is a whole other ballpark. When an athlete gets hurt, the comeback can feel like climbing a mountain without knowing how high it goes. That's why rehab psychology emphasizes **shared goal setting**: breaking recovery into small, measurable milestones that make progress visible and motivation sustainable.

Milestone Templates

- *Phase 1 (Stabilization)*: "I can lift my leg without pain."
- *Phase 2 (Mobility)*: "I completed a full range-of-motion drill."
- *Phase 3 (Strength)*: "I hit 80% of my pre-injury load on a basic exercise."
- *Phase 4 (Sport-Specific)*: "I did my first full practice drill."
- *Phase 5 (Return-to-Play)*: "I completed a scrimmage without hesitation."

Each stage builds the belief that you can produce the results you aim for. Ticking off small goals gives your brain the boost that says, "I'm getting better."

Return Milestones

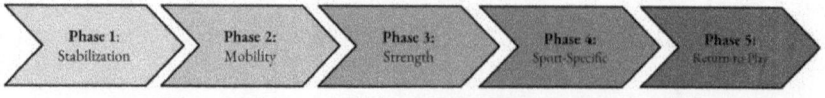

Goal setting isn't enough. You have to *celebrate* progress, too. Rehab can feel repetitive and lonely, so small celebrations act as emotional fuel. It might be as simple as taking a photo at each milestone, writing a quick 'win log,' or sharing progress with your team. Coaches and parents can even set mini-celebration rituals, like an encouraging video from teammates when you finish a phase or a new wristband marking your next step.

Remember:

Don't compare your recovery speed to anyone else's. Every body and injury is unique. What matters is consistency and honesty with your support team.

Finally, communication holds the process together. A clear loop between clinician, coach, athlete, and parent prevents confusion and frustration.

Everyone should know:

1. The current phase of rehab.
2. What the athlete *can* and *can't* do safely.
3. The next milestone goal.

Imagery and Neural Rehearsal During Downtime

Your body may be sidelined, but your mind isn't. Weinberg and Gould (2019) present research showing that **mental imagery** (also called **neural rehearsal**) helps injured athletes maintain their game intelligence and keep their brain-body connection alive.

Visualization involves firing many of the same neural pathways as actual movement. That's why elite athletes use imagery to maintain timing, rhythm, and anticipation *even when injured*. You're not "pretending." You're training your brain to stay fluent in your sport.

Sport-Specific Imagery Sequences

Close your eyes and mentally run through a regular training session:

- See the environment.
- Feel the sensations.
- Hear the sounds.

For example, a soccer player imagines trapping the ball, scanning the field, and making a precise pass.

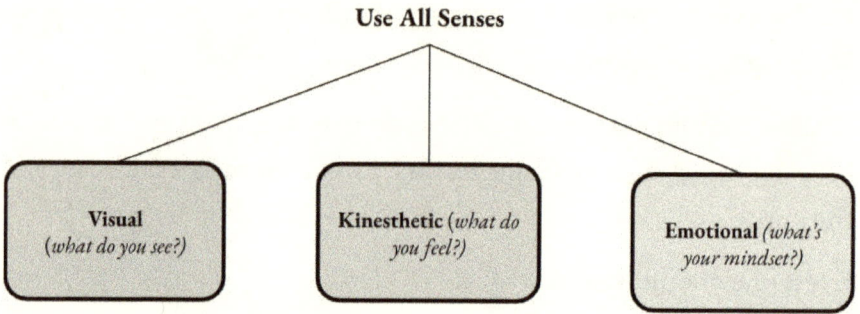

Pair Imagery with Light Movement

If your rehab plan allows it, add micro-movements, like shifting weight or miming a movement in slow motion. This combination keeps motor pathways alive and reduces the "rust" that builds up from complete disuse.

For example, a basketball player rehabbing an ankle might visualize a jump shot while flexing the uninjured leg, syncing rhythm and timing without pressure.

Stage-Based Imagery Scripts

You can tailor this visualization to each rehab phase:

- ***Early Stage***: Focus on calm breathing and visualizing healing. Picture your tissue repairing and swelling decreasing.
- ***Middle Stage***: Visualize specific rehab exercises being done smoothly, in a controlled manner, and pain-free.

- **Late Stage**: Run through complete plays or drills at game speed in your mind, anticipating scenarios and decisions.

Writing out your own imagery "scripts" helps you stay consistent. Start with five minutes a day, building to 10–15 minutes. Pair it with journaling or short reflection prompts ("What did I see clearly today? What felt most real?"), building **psychological readiness** even before you're cleared to play.

Psychological Readiness Checklist

Physical clearance doesn't automatically mean you're mentally ready. True readiness includes emotional confidence, decision speed, sleep quality, and pain management skills. In fact, many athletes reinjure themselves not because their bodies weren't ready, but because their minds weren't yet aligned.

1. *Confidence*

A confident athlete plays fluidly; a hesitant one plays tight and at risk.

- Do you trust the injured area?
- Can you perform without constantly thinking about it?

2. *Emotional Regulation*

Emotional resilience can be rebuilt through visualization, gradual exposure, and self-talk cues such as "strong and stable" or "trust your training."

Do you feel:

- calm under pressure
- anxious and fearful

3. *Sleep Quality*

Recovery neural as well. Poor sleep slows coordination, reaction time, and emotional control. Track your consistency for at least a week before returning.

4. Decision Speed

Hesitation often signals lingering doubt. Coaches can run 'decision-speed drills,' like small-sided games or reactive cues, to test this safely.

- During practice, are your reactions automatic again?

5. Pain Management

Are you able to distinguish between:

- Safe discomfort (normal effort)
- Warning pain (injury risk)

Understanding that difference keeps you proactive.

Red Flags for Poor Adjustment to Injury:

- Being angry or confused constantly
- Obsessing over when you can return
- Denial ("It's not a big deal," "I wasn't hurt that bad.")
- Insisting on coming back too soon (risking re-injury)
- Exaggerating accomplishments and skills pre-injury
- Feeling guilty, or like you disappointed your team/coach/parents
- Isolating yourself
- Mood swings
- Pessimism and dejection ("I'm never going to get better.")

If the athlete is displaying any of the above signs (or things to that effect), then they're most likely *not* psychologically ready to get back into play. In that case, continue working on mindset exercises, goal setting, visualization, and support until they feel ready.

Controlled Scrimmage Ramp-Ups

Once you get through the checklist, understand that rehab doesn't jump from solo drills to full games overnight.

It needs to follow a **graded exposure plan**:

- *Step 1*: Individual skills at moderate intensity.
- *Step 2*: Controlled 1-v-1 or 2-v-2 situations.
- *Step 3*: Small scrimmage with time/space limits.
- *Step 4*: Full practice with monitoring.

This progressive return helps your reintegration become smooth, minimizing overload and re-injury risk.

Communication Plan

Return-to-play decisions work best when everyone's aligned. You, your coach, your physio, and your parents should agree on:

- Clear progress markers.
- Red flags for regression (like swelling, fatigue, or anxiety spikes).
- How feedback is shared (texts, logs, weekly check-ins).

When communication flows, you can feel safer and more respected, and everyone can be much more confident in the comeback plan.

Burnout Prevention and Life Transitioning

Burnout builds quietly, without you realizing, until it suddenly crashes onto you. One week, you're pumped to train and get back on the horse;

the next, you're dragging yourself to practice, wondering why you can't find the passion for the sport you love so much. Rehab psychology research shows that physical and mental recovery share the same rule:

You can't heal what you don't notice.

The first step to burnout prevention is catching early signals.

Early Signals and Load Management

So, what should you watch out for? Look for **behavior indicators**:

- Snapping at teammates
- Zoning out during drills
- Losing interest in hobbies you used to love
- Feeling "foggy."
- Having a shorter fuse
- No longer caring about goals that once motivated

None of these is a sign of weakness. They're just a 'check engine' light for your brain, reminding you to slow down, not overwork yourself, and that burnout might be around the corner.

As soon as you spot these red flags, quick schedule tweaks can save the day. You're not going to *quit* or stop. You're going to *adjust*. Maybe you shorten a few sessions, focus on technique rather than intensity, or swap a high-pressure competition for a fun scrimmage. This way, you're **managing your load**. **Load management** is balancing the stress you take on (both mental and physical) with the recovery you allow yourself.

The Micro De-load Week

This is a helpful tool that consists of a short, planned downshift in training intensity every few weeks. You're giving your body and brain a pit stop *before* the tank hits empty, so it doesn't suddenly crash and burn.

During these micro de-loads, you could shift the focus to mobility, breathwork, reflection, composure training, or tactical video review rather than heavy reps or sprints. You're recharging while staying engaged.

Coach-Parent Agreement

Communication matters too. When adults coordinate, it creates a safety net for you. This can include setting agreed-upon rest windows, discussing school demands, and reviewing mental health cues. This avoids the tough spot of feeling trapped between coach expectations and family life; now, everyone's working together as *one* support team.

Coach-Parent Agreement

Coach:_____

Parent/Guardian:_____

Athlete:_____

Date:_____

We all agree that:

- [Athlete]'s health and happiness come first, before wins, rankings, or stats.
- Progress is measured by growth and effort, not outcome.
- Communication is open and respectful.

Weekly Check-Ins: Every_____ (review practice hours, school

tests, travel).

Rest Day per Week:_____

Micro-Deload Week: Every 4–6 weeks, intensity is reduced by 20–30%.

Peak Windows:_____

No-Pressure Phases:_____

Off-Season Recovery:_____

Notes:

- During exams, training time may be reduced without penalty.
- Family commitments are respected as part of [ATHLETE]'s well-being.
- [ATHLETE] never trains through pain.
- "Are you still having fun?" is a standard question.
- Zero tolerance for burnout/emotional exhaustion. Reset and revisit priorities.

Building Multiple Identities

What often happens in youth sports is **over-investment**: when your identity becomes entirely wrapped around being *'the athlete.'* That might sound fine when things are going well, but what about when there's an injury? A tough season? The day the sports journey will inevitably end? Sport psychology warns us that when athletes lose the activity that defines them, they tend to struggle with motivation, self-worth, and direction.

That's why you need to *build multiple identities.*

You are more than your stats or medals. You're a teammate, a student, a musician, a gamer, a big brother/sister, a friend, a volunteer, and more. Having more than one *you* helps protect your happiness when one part of life takes a dip.

Start by exploring other passions and skills. These could be related to your sport—helping younger players as a junior coach or designing a fitness app with a friend—or entirely unrelated, like taking a photography class. Don't think of these as "distractions" from your training. You're expanding *who you are*. Research shows that having multiple interests strengthens creativity and your sense of self. You bring ideas from one area into another, and suddenly, you're solving problems differently, both on and off the field.

When you hit a life transition, like recovering from an injury, graduating high school/college, or shifting away from competition, try thinking about **transition pathways**:

Do you want to step into coaching or mentoring, helping others learn from your lessons?

Do you want to focus on study schedules that open doors to sports science, psychology, physiotherapy, or media?

All these options are why coaches (and athletes) should develop a life skills module. Through this, you can learn simple tools to handle both daily structure and long-term planning. Learn time management on a grander scale than just your workout regimen, or goal setting beyond the season, or career prep basics. Use planners, habit trackers, and weekly energy audits for all aspects of your life, not just sports. Simply filling your schedule isn't the goal; it's about designing a life that fits your values and your training.

Remember: Burnout thrives when life feels one-dimensional.

Post-Adversity Growth and Meaning Making

You are going to face setbacks. That's just the reality that every athlete has to go through. It might be a season-ending injury, getting benched, or missing a key opportunity. Bouncing back sounds excellent, but so does bouncing *forward*.

Step 1: Narrative Reconstruction

Basically, you rewrite your story so that it makes sense of the struggle. "I lost everything" becomes "I learned what really drives me."

Other prompts are:

- *"What did this challenge teach me about myself?"*
- *"How can I use what I learned to help someone else?"*
- *"What parts of me got stronger through this?"*
- *"Which traits did I discover that I didn't know I had?"*
- *"What advice would I give my past self on the first day of this setback?"*

This isn't about pretending things are fine. You're finding meaning in the setback and using it for growth.

Step 2: Team Integration Rituals

When you share lessons from your struggles, you create a team culture where challenges are normalized rather than suppressed. Some teams hold 'resilience circles' where players share what they've learned from challenging moments. Others create wall boards or digital journals where teammates write reflections or shout-outs to people who overcame something difficult.

Step 3: Reflective Practices

To sustain your growth momentum in the long term, build these reflective practices into your routine. Every month, take ten minutes to look back at how far you've come:

- *"What new skills or mindsets am I proud of?"*
- *"Where do I still get triggered by old frustrations?"*
- *"What habits keep me grounded?"*
- *"How do I celebrate milestones, whether physical or emotional?"*
- *"What new direction or dream has opened up?"*
- *"What parts of me stayed strong, even during the hardest days?"*
- *"How do my experiences change what I value in my sport and life?"*

Through combining psychological first aid, injury recovery, and burnout prevention, you survive your sport *and* evolve through it. You learn how to listen to your body, protect your energy, and redefine success beyond wins and losses.

Passion is a fire that needs air as well as constant fuel. Giving yourself recovery and reflection makes your drive sustainable and your growth balanced.

Key Takeaways

- Injury is both a physical setback *and* a psychological crossroads. Calm containment prevents chaos and panic, while inclusion preserves your identity and keeps things in perspective.
- Rehab psychology and recovery from injury are about the hundreds of small intentional steps you take, along with celebrating how frustration turns into progress. This involves micro-goals, communication, and keeping your mind active even when your body rests.

- Managing your load, burnout prevention through early signals, diversifying your identity, and finding meaning in setbacks form a cycle that keeps you mentally healthy and motivated in the long run.

Champion Mantra:

"A comeback is not luck; it's the roadmap you write while injured."

Conclusion: From Blueprint to Daily Practice

You've just done something many athletes never do: built a complete mental training system.

What started as a couple of motivation tips is now a complete blueprint for focusing, staying calm, rebuilding confidence, and turning setbacks into comebacks. However, a blueprint means nothing unless it becomes a *daily practice*.

This conclusion is your launch pad. The following steps show you that mental toughness is measurable, trainable, and 100% within your control.

Let's look back at the journey you had:

- You learned the language of mental training, what mental toughness *actually* is, how to measure progress, and why ethics and self-awareness matter.

- You discovered how pre-performance routines and constraint-led games sharpen focus naturally, practicing switching between narrow and broad attention.

- You mapped your arousal curve, learned to read your own signals, and used breath anchors to stay centered under stress.

- You built mastery logs to document progress, rewrote negative self-talk scripts, and explored narrative identity.

- You understood that real motivation comes from autonomy, competence, and relatedness, and that building season systems breaks big goals into small milestones.

- You learned to stack habits, manage your nutrition, optimize sleep, and protect your recovery.

- You trained perception using ecological dynamics, showing how adaptive decisions emerge from realistic, constraint-led training.

- Finally, you faced setbacks head-on, learning psychological first aid, how to rebuild confidence during rehab, and how to extract growth from adversity.

Now, it's time to put together everything you've learned. Remember those three short drills (the **Micro Start**) you learned right after the introduction?

- *Reset*: 3 deep breaths + 1 focus cue word.

- *Pre-Training Ritual*: Quick goal statement + visualization + anchor breath.

- *Evening Reflection*: Write one thing learned + one thing improved.

Have you been doing them every day? Maybe you haven't, and that's okay. That was just a test drive. The action has begun.

The 30-Day Micro Start

Either use these drills (or pick your top three micro-drills from the book).

Do them every single day for 30 days. No excuses.

You can use the printable calendar in the appendices to check off or color in a box for each goal achieved after each session. That will be your proof of discipline. By the end, you'll have 90 data entries (3 goals x 30 days) that you can follow through and learn from.

Team Adoption: The Two-Week Pilot

If you're part of a team, this is where your leadership can shine. Suggest a 2-week mental skills pilot program where everyone commits to a daily 3-minute drill.

For example:

- Breathing exercise before warm-ups
- Post-practice gratitude check

Keep it light and curious. Then, of course, reflect and ask your teammates:

- *"What drill made practice feel smoother?"*
- *"Who noticed their focus shift?"*

After two weeks, collect the reflections and decide which drills to keep. This way, your mental training has become a shared language, transforming your team culture into one that grows together.

The 90-Day Roadmap

That 30-Day Micro Start is just month one of your journey. Each month, you're building on the last, so you go from structure to skill to mastery:

Month 1: Structure (Build Micro-Habits)	Month 2: Skill (Layer Systems)	Month 3: Mastery (Track, Reflect, Adjust)
Choose three 3–5 minute drills. Don't overthink it. Just start. Your goal isn't intensity, but consistency. You're writing new neural patterns and proving to yourself that you can show up every day.	Link your micro-drills into a pre-performance system. Add simple feedback loops.	Review the data—notice which drills actually make you feel sharper or calmer. Adjust what doesn't work.
Ex: *#1: Focus Reset Routine* *#2: Breath Anchor* *#3: Mastery Log*	*Pre-Performance System: Breath Anchor → Focus Cue → Self-Talk Script* *Feedback Loop:* *Rate focus (1–5) after practice* *Review the weekly confidence log*	*Adjustment:* *Switch evening reflection for morning visualization.*

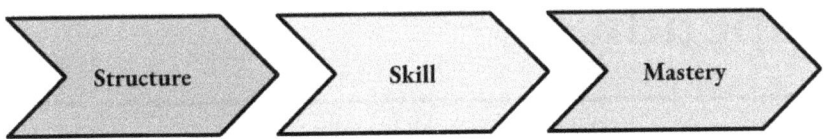

Ultimately, you build toughness, one rep at a time.

Mental toughness is a daily skill. In this book, we helped you build the foundation: focus, emotion control, confidence, motivation, habits, decision-making, and resilience. It's *your* job to live it.

There will be days when you forget a drill or feel tired. That's okay. The secret is in coming back, every time. The more you do, the more your choices and actions will become automatic.

You don't need to be perfect. You just need to start.

Train your mind, for it is unbreakable.

Appendices

Daily Micro-Journal

Name: _____ Date: _____

Sport: _____

1. *Set Your Intentions*

Focus Word/Phrase for Today: _____

Top Goal for Today: _____

Energy Check:
- ☐ Low
- ☐ Okay
- ☐ High

2. *Midday Focus: Stay Grounded*

What am I working on right now? _____

Cue Word or Anchor: _____

- Picture the first action you'll take with full focus.

Readiness:

(1) (2) (3) (4) (5)

3. *Review and Reflect*

1 Win from Today: _____

1 Lesson Learned: _____

1 Gratitude: _____

Confidence Level:

Young Athletes' Blueprint for Mental Toughness

① ② ③ ④ ⑤

Focus Level:

① ② ③ ④ ⑤

Sleep Routine:

- ☐ Power Down Devices
- ☐ Reflect
- ☐ Read
- ☐ Stretch
- ☐ Breathe

End-of-Day Prompt:

Ex: What did I handle better than I would have a month ago?

_____
_____
_____
_____
_____

Printable Focus Cue Cards

Lock In
Eyes on what matters. Turn out the noise.
(Exhale slowly + narrow visual focus)

See Clear
Observe first, decide second.
(Quick blink reset + one deep breath)

In the Zone
One play, one moment, full presence.
(Touch wristband + one inhale)

Own It
I've trained for this. I belong here.
(Stand tall + chest open + breathe in)

Next Rep
Forget the last play. Win this one.
(Quick shake of shoulders)

Breathe Easy
Control your breath, control the game.
(4-count inhale, 4-count exhale)

Center
Return to calm before you react.
(Feel feet grounded + one slow exhale)

Steady
Tension out, rhythm in.
(Shoulder roll + exhale through nose)

Customize Your Cards

Cue Word: _____

Phrase: _____

(Anchor): _____

Cue Word: _____

Phrase: _____

(Anchor): _____

30-Day Micro Start Journal

Name:_____ Sport:_____
Start Date:_____ End Date:_____

Daily Tracking

Day	Drill #1	Drill #2	Drill #3	Focus (1–5)	Confidence (1–5)	Energy (1–5)
1	☐	☐	☐			
2	☐	☐	☐			
3	☐	☐	☐			
4	☐	☐	☐			
5	☐	☐	☐			
6	☐	☐	☐			
7	☐	☐	☐			
Weekly Reflection:	What habit was easiest to stick with? When did I feel most focused or confident? One thing I'll adjust for next week:_____					
8	☐	☐	☐			
9	☐	☐	☐			
10	☐	☐	☐			
11	☐	☐	☐			

Young Athletes' Blueprint for Mental Toughness

12	☐	☐	☐			
13	☐	☐	☐			
14	☐	☐	☐			
Weekly Reflection:	\multicolumn{6}{l}{*How has my mood or energy changed?*}
	\multicolumn{6}{l}{*Which drill feels most effective so far?*}
	\multicolumn{6}{l}{*One obstacle I overcame this week:*_____}
15	☐	☐	☐			
16	☐	☐	☐			
17	☐	☐	☐			
18	☐	☐	☐			
19	☐	☐	☐			
20	☐	☐	☐			
21	☐	☐	☐			
Weekly Reflection:	\multicolumn{6}{l}{*When did I notice improvement in performance or focus?*}
	\multicolumn{6}{l}{*What routine or cue word worked best under pressure?*}
	\multicolumn{6}{l}{*One mindset shift I noticed:*_____}
22	☐	☐	☐			
23	☐	☐	☐			
24	☐	☐	☐			
25	☐	☐	☐			
26	☐	☐	☐			
27	☐	☐	☐			

28	☐	☐	☐			
Weekly Reflection:	*What does 'mental toughness' mean to me now?* *How will I keep this system going after 30 days?* *My next 30-day goal: _____*					
29	☐	☐	☐			
30	☐	☐	☐			

Thank You

Thank you for choosing this book. In a market filled with options, I sincerely appreciate your decision to invest your time here.

Thoughtful reader feedback plays a critical role in maintaining the quality and relevance of independent publishing. If this book met your expectations or provided value, I encourage you to share your experience by leaving a review. Reviews help set accurate expectations for future readers and guide the continued development of work like this.

Your perspective matters, and it directly influences the standard of content I create going forward.

Thank you for reading and for your support.

Resources

Bandura, A. (1997). *Self-efficacy: The Exercise of Control.* W. H. Freeman and Company.

Csikszentmihalyi, M. (1990). *Flow: The Psychology of Optimal Experience.* Harper and Row.

Davids, K., Button, C., & Bennett, S. (2008). *Dynamics of skill acquisition: A constraints-led approach.* Human Kinetics.

Duckworth, A. (2016). *Grit: The power of passion and perseverance.* Scribner.

Dweck, C. S. (2006). *Mindset: The new psychology of success.* Random House. https://adrvantage.com/wp-content/uploads/2023/02/Mindset-The-New-Psychology-of-Success-Dweck.pdf

Kim, H.-G., Cheon, E.-J., Bai, D.-S., Lee, Y. H., & Koo, B.-H. (2018). Stress and Heart Rate Variability: A Meta-Analysis and Review of the Literature. *Psychiatry Investigation, 15*(3), 235–245. https://doi.org/10.30773/pi.2017.08.17

McAdams, D. P., & McLean, K. C. (2013). Narrative Identity. *Current Directions in Psychological Science, 22*(3), 233–238. http://www.jstor.org/stable/44319052

Ryan, R. M., & Deci, E. L. (2000). Self-determination Theory and the Facilitation of Intrinsic Motivation, Social Development, and Well-being. *American Psychologist, 55*(1), 68–78. https://doi.org/10.1037/0003-066X.55.1.68

Walker, M. P. (2017). *Why We Sleep: Unlocking the Power of Sleep and Dreams.* Scribner, An Imprint Of Simon & Schuster, Inc.

Weinberg, R. S., & Gould, D. (2019). *Foundations of sport and exercise psychology* (7th ed.). Human Kinetics.

www.ingramcontent.com/pod-product-compliance
Lightning Source LLC
Chambersburg PA
CBHW032113090426
42743CB00007B/338